In Relation to Relationships

Riemann, Jöst, Fischer, Berchtold

In Relation to Relationships

Intensive pedagogic support under the magnifying glass

Bibliografische Information der Deutschen Nationalbibliothek:
Die Deutsche Nationalbibliothek verzeichnet diese Publikation in der Deutschen Nationalbibliografie; detaillierte bibliografische Daten sind im Internet über http://dnb.dnb.de abrufbar.

© 2013 Name des Autors/Rechteinhabers **Jens (Jenne) Riemann**

Illustration: **Marlies Lüpges (Photo)**
Übersetzung: **Gyles Palmer, Burkhard Ehring, Stefan Baumeister**

Herstellung und Verlag: BoD – Books on Demand, Norderstedt

ISBN: 978-3 7386 0859 5

Table of Contents

Foreword for the English Translation 14

Acknowledgements 16

1. Introduction - Research Design 17
    1.1. Child, youth and family support in Germany 17
    1.2. Background and current research 18
        1.2.1. Summary of the research so far 20
    1.3. The decision to undertake qualitative research 21
    1.4. Subject of the research and original hypothesis 23
    1.5. Survey Method and context 26
        1.5.1. Analysis of Files 27
        1.5.2. Guided Interviews 27
        1.5.3. Group Discussions (German Version) 30
        1.5.4. Sampling 30
        1.5.5. Analysis of the findings 32

2. Case Study André 37
    2.1. Current situation 37
    2.2. Case history 39
    2.3. History 41
    2.4. Initiating Contact / Initial Approach for Help 42
    2.5. Key Themes and goals of the support 43

3.7. Setting design 89

    3.7.1. Care work in the supported living group (SLG) and the emergency accommodation 89

    3.7.2. Transfer to Italy 93

    3.7.3. 1:1 care in Italy 94

    3.7.4. Post programme ambulant support in Germany 97

3.8. The participation of the young person and his parents 99

    3.8.1. Christian's participation 99

    3.8.2. Participation of the parents 104

3.9. The quality of the relationship between the young person and the support services 106

    3.9.1. Christian - ambulant care worker in Germany 106

    3.9.2. Christian - care worker in Italy 109

    3.9.3. Christian - other professionals 112

    3.9.4. Relationships with others 114

3.10. Process design between the young person and the support services 115

    3.10.1. Social behaviour 115

    3.10.2. Emotional maturity 119

    3.10.3. Life skills 123

3.11. Stakeholder collaboration 125

3.12. Conclusion of the programme and ongoing support 126

- 3.13. The impact of the support and its effects as seen by the interviewees 128
  - 3.13.1. Social behaviour 129
  - 3.13.2. Emotional maturity 131
  - 3.13.3. Family relationships.................................. 132
  - 3.13.4. Life skills 132
- 3.14. Christian's ideas for his future.. 135
- 3.15. Summary 135

4. Case Study Lena 139
   - 4.1. Current situation 139
   - 4.2. Case history 140
   - 4.3. History 141
   - 4.4. Initiating Contact / Initiation of support 143
   - 4.5. Key themes and goals of the support............................. 144
     - 4.5.1. Problematic social behaviour 144
     - 4.5.2. Family relationships................................... 145
     - 4.5.3. Emotional maturity 145
     - 4.5.4. Life skills 146
   - 4.6. Resources of the young person and her family 147
     - 4.6.1. Lena's resources 147
     - 4.6.2. Family resources....................................... 148

4.7. Setting design 149

    4.7.1. First location 149

    4.7.2. Transition to Germany 150

    4.7.3. Ambulant after care in Germany 151

4.8. Participation of the young person and her parents 152

    4.8.1. Lena's participation 152

    4.8.2. Participation of the parents 153

4.9. Quality of the relationship between the young person and the support services 153

    4.9.1. Lena - care worker(s) 154

    4.9.2. Lena - coordinator 156

4.10. Process design between young person and the support services 158

    4.10.1. Social behaviour 158

    4.10.2. Emotional maturity 159

    4.10.3. Family relationships 160

    4.10.4. Life skills 162

4.11. Stakeholder collaboration 163

4.12. Conclusion of the programme and ongoing support 164

4.13. The impact of the support and its effects as seen by the interviewees 164

    4.13.1. Social behaviour 165

	4.13.2.	Emotional maturity 167
	4.13.3.	Family relationships.. 168
	4.13.4.	Life skills 169
4.14.		Lena's ideas for her future 170
4.15.		Summary 171
5. Conclusion 173		
5.1.		The caring relationship as foundation and opportunity 173
5.2.		Working with biographies 181
5.3.		Support plans versus themes 183
5.4.		Participation 185
	5.4.1.	Participation of the young people 185
	5.4.2.	Participation by the parents 188
5.5.		Resources and potential 189
	5.5.1.	The young person's resources 189
	5.5.2.	Family resources 191
5.6.		Setting (location and concept of the programme) 194
5.7.		Cooperation amongst stakeholders 196
	5.7.1.	Youth Welfare Office 196
	5.7.2.	Service provider – care worker................................. 196
	5.7.3.	The care worker and other support services / institutions 197

6. A view – aspects of attachment theory in individual social educational (pedagogic) work and research 199

List of references 204

Appendix 1 208

    Guidelines for Interviews 208

        Interview Guideline Adolescents 208

        Interview Guideline Parents 211

        Interview Guideline Care Worker 214

        Interview Guideline Coordination 217

        Interview Guideline Youth Welfare Office 220

The Authors 222

Foreword for the English Translation

"In Relation to Relationships. - Intensive pedagogic support under the magnifying glass"

The research "Beziehungsweise Bindung – Intensivpädagogische Hilfeverläufe unter der Lupe" has been completed as the result of a number of factors.

The first is that the authors work in a number of languages and cultural contexts in Youth Support.

At the same time the interest in intensive pedagogic support is growing in Europe.

Finally, the authors wish to share their work and be involved in the international academic discourse and consultation as well as the exchange of knowledge about intensive pedagogic care for children and adolescents.

The original impetus to undertake this translation is to enable us to provide the German perspective to the conference in June 2015 in Halifax (Canada) "Pathways to resilience III: Beyond nature versus nurture" The thought of being able to participate in this conference is closely related to the conclusions we came to as a result of our evaluation.

The research was developed and informed through interviews with clients (young people), their parents and the care professionals as they expressed their experiences from their own point of views. The aim of the research was to identify what characteristics of the interventions made them successful?

In Germany, this study is at the moment the first qualitative long-term study of its kind. At the time the interviews took place, the programme run by "Jugendhilfe Phöinix e. V." had finished at least three years previously.

In order to make it possible to complete this translation, the number of case studies used in the original (German version) research was reduced from seven to three; the selected three studies provide good examples that, between them, demonstrate the outcomes of the research.

We hope that our English speaking readers find this research interesting and thought provoking.

Acknowledgements

In order to be able to carry out this research we have been helped by many colleagues

Our first and very special thanks go to the young people, their parents and the Social Workers who were prepared to be interviewed. Without their help, their openness and their trust as well as their flexibility we would not have been able to carry out this project.

Thanks also to the staff of "Jugendhilfe Phöinix e. V." who provided specialist advice and valuable constructive criticism.

We thank Gyles Palmer and Burkhard Ehring for the translation who apologise in advance for any confusion arising out of the translation, especially of quotations. It is suggested that readers refer to the original documents where needed.

1. Introduction - Research Design

1.1. Child, youth and family support in Germany

This research takes place within the legal parameters of German Social legislation which we will briefly explain. This will place the work and the research in context.

The rights and responsibilities of parents for the care and education of their children are laid out in law by the Federal Republic of Germany Constitutional Order (Section 6, Paragraph 2, second sentence). The state is required to ensure that these rights and responsibilities are carried out. In all of its actions, the state must place the welfare of the child over all else.

If the parents are unable to care alone for their children, they have a legal right to support from the state to help them.

It is assumed that the state will play a supportive role and will only use force, for example the removal of the child, if the parents are putting the child's welfare at risk.

The Child and Youth Welfare Act is part of the Social Act (Sozialgesetzbuches VIII) and defines the criteria for eligibility for the provision of help. In order to achieve this, a range of children and youth welfare services have been developed. These include support for organisations such as children's day care services, schools or recreational centres as well as more targeted support for vulnerable young people and their families who are at risk.

Services have become increasingly differentiated and specialised in order to meet this wide range of complex needs.

In principle the support is provided through independent organisations who are contracted to provide services by the Youth Welfare Office (Jugendamt) of the local authority. The state only provides services directly when there is no organisation who is able to provide the specific service required. The partnership between the service provider, the state and the service user is based on close participation of all parties, regardless of age, in the development of the support plan.

If a child or youth can neither be supported in the family nor in an institution, the legislation provides for "Intensive 1:1 social education" (Intensive sozialpädagogische Einzelbetreuung) (§ 35 SGB VIII). The law requires that, if the child or youth is at high risk and there is no appropriate alternative service, then an individual programme should be developed and carried out.

The tailor made service would specify who provides the social education, where it should be provided and the content of the programme.

Our research focussed on these programmes in social education developed for these very individual cases.

1.2. Background and current research

This research, published in Germany in 2014, is the result of experience gathered by staff of Jugendhilfe Phöinix e. V in their work in this area over the last 18 years. During this time over 700 Intensive 1:1 social education programmes were delivered with children and young people in line with this part of the Child and Youth Welfare Act (§ 35 SGB VIII).

Young people who are cared for through this form of intensive support have usually had traumatic experiences. Their biographies record multiple breakdowns and changes and sometimes long careers as the clients of Psychiatric and Youth Services.

Some of the authors of this research now work for "imBlick Kinder- und Jugendhilfe gGmbH" which is a successor to "Jugendhilfe Phöinix e. V." As a result of what was learnt through this research, they plan to carry out a further study which examines in more detail aspects of "Matching of the Care Worker and the Young Person".

The aim of the Intensive 1:1 social education process is to enable the young person to live in an independent and socially acceptable way through the provision of a setting aligned with their needs. The young person should be given the opportunity to experience alternative ways of behaving and thinking and integrating them into their own range of responses.

In the context of the highly differentiated support programmes delivered by "Jugendhilfe Phöinix e. V" the responsible professionals began to ask themselves whether reliance on experience and the belief in current theories was a sufficiently empirical foundation for the design of the programmes.

"Jugendhilfe Phöinix e. V" had established a range of guiding work practices, hypotheses and success factors for intensive social education support (see Chapter 1.3).
In 2008 during a workshop it was suggested that these hypotheses should be tested to see if they were supported through empirical evidence and research.
At that time in Germany, qualitative and quantitative social research began to explore the degree to which intensive social education really worked. Currently, there are a few quantitative as well as qualitative studies available. These include self-evaluations by service providers and more overarching research of the field as a whole, as part of a dissertation. The following explanations are meant to provide an overview of the research design of those studies.

1.2.1. Summary of the research so far

In 2003, Klaus Fröhlich-Gildhoff published a dissertation which explored the concepts, processes and effectiveness of intensive youth work (Einzelbetreuung)[1]. Gildhoff's aim was a "comprehensive picture of the practice of intensive social education in its various forms"[2], in order to identify the elements of the work which led to successful outcomes.[3] He closely examined the relationship between the carer and the child or youth as well as the external conditions.

In 2007, the "Institut des Rauhen Hauses für Soziale Praxis gGmbH" (a partnership between several intensive social education service providers) carried out research into the development of the ability to cope with or master everyday life at school, work, at home and legal behaviour through long term intensive social education in Germany and abroad.

355 participants answered 60 standardised and open questions which were then analysed[4].

Two years later, Torsten Fischer and Jörg Ziegenspeck concentrated on intensive social education outside Germany in qualitative research which aimed to understand the impact of this form of informal learning and experience and whether and what personal characteristics can be taught [5]

At the same time, a dissertation by Matthias Witte described the biographical and social environment of young people in intensive so-

---

1   Fröhlich-Gildhoff 2003

2   Fröhlich-Gildhoff 2003: 24

3   This refers to measurable indicators of the success or failure of an intervention. These might be, for example, an analysis of the early stage, changes during the programme and the core change factors in the intensive care work.

4   AIM e.V. 2007

5   Fischer; Ziegenspeck 2009

cial education programmes outside Germany. He focused on the young people's view of their reality. He did this through the analysis of 12 comprehensive case studies, biographical stories, observation and photo interviews[6].

One year later, Willy Klawe developed a multi perspective reconstruction of the social education process and interventions by involving the workers various stakeholders on the completion of their intervention. Klawe produced 12 case monographs which allowed Klawe to generate, key processes and elements that contribute to the ability to deal successfully with day to day life.

In 2011, the so-called InHAus Studie (individual social education abroad) carried out research using experimental and control groups. Comparisons were made between the effects of intensive social education abroad and supported living in Germany[7].

1.3. The decision to undertake qualitative research

In the final analysis, the senior staff of intensive social education and care at provider "Jugendhilfe Phöinix e. V." decided to undertake evaluation research that was carried out by staff with the help of external consultants between 2010 and 2013.

The hope was to develop a deeper understanding through the eyes of the participants in the process and their decision making during a programme to identify possible key factors impacting on success or failure and to use them to inform one's own work.

The object of the research can be best described as Individual Education. Each intervention is unique to the individual person in content,

---

6   Witte 2009

7   Klein; Arnold; Mascenaere 2011

method, staffing and area. No two programmes are alike. Since the programmes could not be standardised, it was not possible to gather quantitative data and therefore the team chose qualitative research.

"The ambition of qualitative research is to describe the world in terms of the subjective experience of the participants. This will achieve a better understanding of the social reality(ies) of the participants and help us identify actions and consequences, patterns of meaning and structural characteristics"[8].

"By mostly using narrative, the qualitative research method allows a more open way of gathering data about the exploration of the research subject which in turn contributes to achieving a more multidimensional, graphic and concrete picture of the situation from the perspective of the people concerned[9]"

In order to deal with the subject adequately, the research team decided that they would reconstruct and analyse a few specific cases, in particular the participants' perceptions of reality and interpretive frames (theory of the world).

First, the cases would be examined in detail and individually and in the second step, they would be compared to identify similarities. The research changed in character from simply being an attempt to test hypotheses about existing practices and performance indicators to a more open study. Now the focus was on using an inductive process of examination to discover something new or interesting or, after a systematic comparison of the cases relevant data, some commonalities.

The resulting research therefore takes into account the constructivist understanding of reality which defines a qualitative approach to evaluation in the sense that social reality is understood as:

---

8 Flick u.a. 2010: 14

9 cp. Flick u.a. 2010: 17

"[...] the result of agreed structures of interactive communication which results in patterns of meaning and behaviour, dialogue and social representation. The reflective and causal nature of their reality would be captured through the qualitative research of the perspective of the participants and their roles and positions. The scientific interpretation itself becomes part of the reconstructive discovery and formation process of the social reality which is the subject of the change of the topic that is being evaluated." [10]

As a result "Jugendhilfe Phöinix e. V." undertook a wide ranging longitudinal research project over a period of four years. This process allowed participation by the staff of Phöinix through feedback into the research process[11]

Regular team meetings provided the opportunity for staff to critique the questions, assumptions and evaluation criteria of the research so far and to develop their own professional skills.

As a result inferences could be made about the appropriateness of the particular professional practices in a specific intensive social education interventions. As a result of the open research design and as the programme progressed, these new inferences could be applied in practice.

1.4. Subject of the research and original hypothesis

Through an open and explorative process the research seeks to find insights into the following **question**:

How does "Jugendhilfe Phöinix e. V", support young people with traumatic and multiple experiences of failed youth welfare interven-

---

10 Wilson zit in: v. Kardorff 2010: 244-245

11 v. Kardorff 2010: 246

tions live a life which is both acceptable to them and to the society they live in?

The **working hypothesis** was as follows:

Intensive social education programmes can provide the greatest possible support to young people with traumatic experiences and multiple experience of failed youth welfare interventions to live a life which is both acceptable to them and to the society they live in when they programmes cater for them as individuals. These individually relevant settings offer them new experiences and alternative concepts and ways of behaving and the newly learned behaviours can then be integrated into the young peoples' lives.

The question then arises as to what are the characteristics which could be considered to be most important in a successful programme? The research team agreed on the following criteria:

1. That the young person is assessed as requiring and is provided with an appropriately individualised Setting (care staff, communication, opportunities, environment, contact with the community...) and a relationship between the Care Worker and the young person that will be supportive in enabling them to master the issues they face and promote their self-development.
2. The Young Person's resources
3. The Family's resources
4. Less negative biographical experiences

If the young person has had some of the following experiences, we speak of a very negative biography:

- Neglect (lack of emotional and physical care)
- Experience of abuse (personal or witnessed, psychological or physical, attempted suicide)
- Chronic drug misuse by parents with the result that the child is unable to predict parent behaviour.
- Parents with mental health issues
- Personal experience of drug misuse
- - Long and varied career in the youth welfare and psychiatric health system

When, as a child, the young person has experienced a home / place which was dependable, trusted and providing privacy then we would assess the biographical experience as being less negative.

5. Low referral age

    The earlier a child starts with an intensive social education programme (intensiv-sozialpädagogische Einzelbetreuung ISE), the better is the prognosis for success because specific patterns have not had time to harden. On the other hand, the more resources and emotional resilience a young person has, the more likely it is that they can start later in life.

6. **Support Plans and implementation** (preparation, transition, termination and post programme support)

7. **Participation of the Young Person and their Parents/Carers**

These criteria led to an initial focus on the following case specific elements:

- Biographical experience / history
- The situation of the Young Person and their parents/carers at the beginning of the programme, initial situation, problems, themes, resources
- Support plan and implementation (preparation, transition, termination, post project support) decision making and participation processes.
- The Setting (Match between the Young person and the offer made by the Care Worker)
- The development of relationships and interventions
- Family work
- Cooperation between the Care worker, the professional advisors of the organisation, Youth Office and other stakeholders
- Impact, transfer, situation today

1.5. Survey Method and context

We agreed that the basis of the research would be through case studies as these would most suitable for research subjects with high levels of individuality and would allow a more explorative approach.

"(Case studies) aim to reconstruct or describe a specific case exactly. People, communities (e.g. families), organisations or institutions

(e.g. nursing homes) can be the subject of analysis through case studies. The crucial problem is to identify the cases which provide the strongest examples, the resolution, the context and which methodological approaches are required to reconstruct them"[12]

We used a variety of methods to secure the findings In order to ensure that they were valid.

1.5.1. Analysis of Files

The files enabled us to establish (as far as possible) the history and context and a timeline for the programme. We used case notes, minutes of support plan meetings, reports, assessments, notes, memos and letters.
The information results were recorded in specially developed forms (Appendix 2 and 3, see German version).

The close study of the files also prepared us for the following interviews and helped the interviewer to approach the themes and experiences of the interviewee with a sensitivity appropriate to their experience.
Finally, the analysis of the files allowed conclusions to be drawn about the way the files were managed by the service provider and highlighted areas where improvements could be made.

1.5.2. Guided Interviews

For practical reasons a, mostly, open ended, standardised interview questions were used. This was out of scholarly interest and because it reduced the amount of time required to analyse the data given the limited resources of the research team.

---

12   Flick 2010: 254

The interview consisted of a sequence of, in the most cases, fixed questions which related to the assumed success factors but were kept intentionally open.

The way in which the questions were formulated could be dependent on the specific case and the themes varied. The questions were formulated in a way to encourage narrative so that narrative and active listening (by the interviewer) predominated. The aim of this method was to enable the interviewee to speak freely and develop their own stories within the boundaries set by the questions.

At the end of the interview both parties were given the opportunity to supplement what they had said or talk about other things. ("Are there any other questions that I haven't asked you but that you would have liked to answer?").

The interview was guided and modified for each type of interviewee (young person, parent, carer, specialist advisers, youth service case managers) (Appendix 1).

A pre-test was carried out with each interview and this informed the way in which each interview was carried out.

Carrying out the Interviews

Our aspiration was to interview all of those involved with supporting the young people who are the subject of these case studies. It was possible to interview the young people, the Carers and the Specialist adviser in all of the seven of the cases in the original German publication. We also sought to interview Case managers and parents but this was not always possible because, either the person was not available or not willing to be involved.

The interviews took place between June 2010 and September 2011. A last interview was carried out in December 2012. The interviews were carried out almost entirely face to face using a dictaphone and very occasionally over the telephone.

The seven Case Studies generated 32 interviews;

Young People	7
Parents	4
Carers	9
Coordinators/specialist advisers	9
Youth Service Case Managers	3

In the English version three of the original seven case studies are included.

Record of interviews

In the original German version only those verbal behaviours were recorded that would be analysed.

All interviews were transcribed exactly as spoken. In order to make it easier to understand in this translation most extraneous words were removed.

Behaviour other than speaking may be recorded like this	[laughed] [sighed]
Words which are emphasised are	underlined
Short pauses	..;
Longer pauses	...

We have tried to ensure that the text is legible and approximates the conversation held. Every interview was proof heard and read by a second person in order to avoid mistakes in transcription.

Finally, the names of all participants and locations were anonymised.

1.5.3. Group Discussions (German Version)

Three of the seven case studies were evaluated by a group of staff from "Jugendhilfe Phöinix e. V." who were invited to contribute to the brain storming session as part of a group discussion.

The participants were able to freely express their thoughts and associations with regard to the interviews. Over and above this questions and comments were shared. The discussion was recorded and transcripts made. The findings were taken into account in the steps in the evaluation.

1.5.4. Sampling

The samples were taken from six typical intensive social education programmes with the following criteria:

- Type of support (ambulant or residential)
- Age at start of programme (high: older than 15, low: under 15 years old)
- Care/Programme delivered inside or outside Germany

In the following combinations;

a) Ambulant support and high age of entry to the programme
b) Ambulant support and low age of entry to the programme
c) Residential Programme in or outside Germany and high age entry to the programme

d) Residential Programme in or outside Germany and low age entry to the programme

e) Mixture of ambulant care in Germany and residential care in and outside Germany with high age entry

f) Mixture of ambulant care in Germany and residential care in and outside Germany with low age entry

The completion of the programme must have been at least three years before the beginning of the research to enable us to identify any long term outcomes.

A random sample was taken from each of six groups based on the above criteria, each group had between three and eight cases.

However we found that in some of the sampled cases it was not possible to establish the contact details for all of the participants in the programme delivery. This then became a further criteria for sample selection.

The last criteria was that the young person, their care worker and the professional adviser would be prepared to participate.

Initial contacts took place by telephone and the interviewer explained the aim of the research and the participant confirmed that they would participate.

Ultimately the following case studies were chosen and these broadly cover the spectrum of programmes offered by "Jugendhilfe Phöinix e. V."

Name	Gender	High Age yes/no	Age	Programme
André (a)	male	yes	15 yrs, 11 mths	ambulant programme
Lara (a)	female	yes	18 yrs, 5 mths	ambulant programme
Marvin (b)	male	no	10 yrs, 9 mths	ambulant programme
Lena (c)	female	yes	18 yrs, 10 mths	residential programme
Sebastian (d)	male	no	13 yrs, 1 mth	residential inside & outside Germany
Christian (e)	male	yes	15 yrs, 1 mth	residential inside & outside Germany

| Katja (f) | female | no | 14 yrs, 5 mths | residential inside & outside Germany |

We chose two young people for category (a) because they showed different characteristics: André began the programme at the age of 16 and lived on the street and in a hotel during the programme and Lara lived in her own flat while she was in a programme. The two settings are so different that it was decided to include both of them.

For this translation we have selected the cases of André, Christian und Lena (bold print in table above). This was to achieve a representative range of cases with regard to residential and ambulant care in and outside Germany.

André models the possibilities and limits of a completely ambulant intensive social educational programme. The cases of Lena and Christian give an impression of a programme which is made up of a continuum of ambulant and residential interventions both inside and outside Germany. The criteria for the age of entry to a programme was not prioritised and all of the selected young people were at least 15 at the beginning of the programme.

1.5.5. Analysis of the findings

The way in which we analysed the findings were appropriate to "the open nature of the theoretical hypotheses which initiated the research as well as its "explicit intentions" [13] (Chapter 1.3) and is based on practical research requirements.

We agree with Schmidt that the analysis of guided interviews should "seek unique and pertinent paths"[14]

The chosen analysis techniques are briefly described below:

---

13 Schmidt 2010: 447

14 l.c.: 447 ff.

a) Brainstorming phase

The four person research team read all of the Case interviews. During a brainstorming session the first associations and striking and important features were shared and discussed. This resulted in a number of themes and questions. The minutes of this discussion formed the preparation for later classification. Supplementary groups of colleagues looked in detail at individual cases and the outcomes of these discussions also informed the categorisation.

b) The development of evaluations categories

To begin with, a single interview text was used by the research team to establish categories inductively. Each member of the team did this individually and then shared their conclusions and decided which were most significant and how they should be formulated. These categories were then applied to the next two cases in teams of two people who, after looking at them individually again compared their results with each other. The categories identified were then evaluated and professionally reviewed by the whole team, they were systemised and coding guidelines developed.

These were made up of main and sub categories and were used to analyse the remaining interviews. The final draft of the evaluation grid is contained in Appendix 3.

c) Coding the interviews

Using this grid the interviews were recorded sentence by sentence or even word for word in that the statements were classified according to the categories. The summary of each evaluation contained individual interpretations as well as summary of the content, questions and comments about the coding as well as a reference to the source.

d) The development of the case analysis

The case analysis was developed on the basis of the evaluation grid and the existing attempts at interpretation.

A team of two people, an author and a co-author was formed to consider each case. They oriented their work on the existing structure of the Case analysis.

1. Description of the actual situation of the young person at the time of interview.

2. Biographical history based on files and the personal view of the young person.

3. Description of the central themes and development needs which needed to be met

    a. Problematic social behaviour;
        - A danger to others through violence, aggression,
        - potential to commit crimes,
        - weak social skills (conflict avoidance, introversion, fear of social situations, promiscuity, inappropriate behaviour),

    b. Lack of Life skills e.g.
        - school, training, employment,
        - accommodation,
        - recreation,
        - planning for the future

    c. Integration in the family e.g.
        - Contact to family
        - Role of the family in their development

- Resolution of family conflicts or traumatic experiences (e.g. death, loss)
  d. Lack of maturity e.g.
    - Regressive tendencies
    - Repetition of childlike behaviour
    - Emotional maturity
4. Reconstruction of the programme
5. Description of the process of transfer under the following aspects;
   a. personal and family resources
   b. support plans
      - Preparation
      - Aim of the support
      - The setting
      - Participation by the young person and their relatives
      - The quality of the relationships between the participants
      - Tailoring of interventions to the prioritised themes and development aims
      - Ending of the programme and transitional support

6. Outcome of the programme from the view of the young person and the support team

e) Comparisons of all case studies

In conclusion the research team carried out a comparison of all of the findings from the seven case studies to identify commonalities and differences. This method enabled the team to move from individual views to more general conclusions and features. At the same time these generalisations allowed the cases to be viewed with a deeper understanding, to identify specific features and hypotheses to be tested.

The synopsis of the case studies in this English translation contains a systematic account of these comparisons in full. Changes have only been made in the choice of the examples so that they come only from the case studies of André, Christian und Lena.

2. Case Study André

Sources:
- Case File analysis
- Interviews with:
  - André (André)
  - Care Worker (BE Werner M.)
  - Coordinator (KO Mr. T.)
  - Child's father (KV Mr. R.)
  - Case Worker – Youth Welfare Office (JA Mrs. K.)
  - Care Worker (Ulrike O.)

2.1. Current situation

André now lives in his own rented apartment and has a regular part-time job at a hotel: *"I get up at four-thirty am, go to work at six clock and work until half past one, one" (André 8-9).* He regularly goes to football training. He has difficulty accessing further or higher education because he did not complete high school. He is currently trying to gain his high school qualification at the community college. There is no evidence of criminal activity.

> *"He is trying to gain his high school qualification at the community college but I don't really believe he will do it. He is only going because he is paid to go" (KV Mr. R. 446-447).*

Andre says that his relationship with his father is stable *"Well, my father and I have a super relationship" (André 269)* but his Care Worker makes a more critical assessment:

> *"He spends almost every day with his father, who picks him up by car, and drives him from pillar to post, with him sitting there feeling cool" (BE Werner M. 591-593),*
>
> *"I think this is that moment in the relationship when the son is cared for via the Audi (Car)." (BE Werner M. 596-597)*
>
> *"André still needs to fill out his applications alone, in fact his father leaves him hanging with those sort of things." (BE Werner M. 598-599)*

Having said that, André has many friends and is happy to be out and about "I'm in the football club and train twice a week and if there is no training, I go to my friends to chat and so on, I'm somebody who's out and about a lot." (André 10-13).

2.2. Case history

Sources:	Case Files, Interviews
Start of treatment:	15.12.2004
Age at entry:	15 years 9 months
Termination of support:	28.02.2007
Duration of the ISE:	2 yrs 2months

Care notes

15.12.2004 to 21.02.2005:
Outpatient care - defined clarification (Clearing in deutsch) André and his father 15h / week

15.01.2005 to 15.02.2005:
Full time inpatient in a Project in Germany with additional outpatient care

17.02.2005 to early April 2005:
André lived in Agnesheim (Child Welfare Centre), with outpatient care provided by "Jugendhilfe Phöinix e. V." beginning with 15hrs per week, then 5 hours per week until he moved to live in a hotel in early April 2005

18.05.2005 to 28.02.2007:
Outpatient care for André and his father at the hotel or on the street. Towards the end in Andrés own apartment with 108 hours per month

After an outpatient preparatory phase for André and his father of about 3 months, he was moved to a "Site project" in Germany provided by "Jugendhilfe Phöinix e. V." but this was ended after a relatively short time (approximately one month). Neither of the interviewees gave exact reasons for this.

> "I knew that André had lived at a "Site project" before he moved to the hotel. He lived with my colleague H. and the situation had escalated there. Also, André told me that he had been in many youth welfare measures preceding then. That made it clear for us that he couldn't stay in a group setting and would have to live elsewhere" (KO Mr. T. 7-11).
>
> "The situation in the Site Project was just too close, much too close, and André couldn't deal with it" (KO Mr. T. 27-28).

Following this André returned to a hotel and was provided with intensive and prolonged outpatient care which was shared by a female and a male Care Worker. There were ongoing problems with the accommodation and Andre was expelled from the hotel and returned to the child welfare centre, then back to the hotel or to living on the street. The male worker remained consistent throughout the entire time. The female Care Worker left after about a year because of problems of cooperation between the two Care Workers.

Despite Andre's high level of delinquency and aggression during this time (he made press headlines as a result of Train surfing, throwing rocks at an ICE *[rem: German express train]* and threatening others with knives etc.) it was still possible for the Care Workers to maintain a relationship and continue his outpatient care.

Finally, an apartment was found for André which he was able to maintain for a longer period of time but he continued to show repeated delinquent and criminal behaviour.

Legal representation was found for André prior to the cessation of his outpatient care because the service had the view that in some situations he was unable to act responsibly. This came into force when he was 18 years old. André is still in contact with his Care Worker today.

2.3. History

After André's mother died of cancer in 1994 when he was 5 years old, he was brought up by his single father and his older brother in a deprived area of his hometown.

His father had a full time job and had no support from his family. André was often cared for by his brother who was six years older than himself. *"His brother Alex, who was bigger, he helped me a lot"* (KV Mr. R. 406-407).

Later André's father found a new girlfriend and they lived in her house with her children. When André's behaviour became increasingly aggressive and dangerous (train surfing and other criminal acts), he was provided with a range of youth welfare services, youth protection services, day services and a variety of supported living groups from 2003 on. He occasionally received treatment in psychiatric hospitals.

André had difficulty with group living and was moved from one group to the other. *"None of these stays lasted for very long because André was a very aggressive and difficult young person who often ignored group rules or group norms"* (JA Mrs. K. 25-27).

André was described as aggressive, delinquent and incapable of living in a group. He described himself *"To be clear I was lazy and couldn't be bothered to do anything."* (André 68-69) André couldn't live with his father either, who was scared that he would lose his flat because he couldn't control André.

"He was very rebellious and the neighbours refused to accept it after while" (KV Mr. R. 100-101).

The father felt completely out of his depths and couldn't handle André at all *"because I was totally overwhelmed by the boy"* (KV Mr. R. 67-68).

The Care Worker initially described André in the following way: *"André had no awareness of limits, he gave a shit about any boundary, he only ever travelled without paying, he was a criminal."* (BE Werner M. 103-105).

André was referred to a special school for children with a learning disability. The Youth Welfare Office case history (report Youth Welfare Office 05/05/04) mentions a borderline intellectual disability but no assistance to integration was provided because behavioural problems and not educational deficits were a priority.

André and his father had a very tense relationship *"That was a catastrophe; it was like... it was like slaughter, you know, we really hated each other's guts"* (André 282-283).

The Care Worker talks about the *"affronting behaviour and asocial structures of his father"* (BE Werner M. 123-124). *"André was an unloved child for years and his older brother was the favourite son"* (BE Werner M. 191-192). There were other familial relationships with his brother and his stepmother although the relationship with the latter was very unreliable. *"She tried to take on the mother role but, in principle her emotions were completely unstable"* (BE Werner M. 214-216).

2.4. Initiating Contact / Initial Approach for Help

The advisory board of the Youth Welfare Office dealing with particularly difficult cases recommended outpatient care and therapeutic interventions from "Jugendhilfe Phöinix e. V.". The first goal was to motivate Andre to undertake an intensive educational support programme. At the time, André lived in the Child Welfare Centre and a male and a female Care Worker from "Jugendhilfe Phöinix e. V." made contact with him.

"He lived for a time in our Child Welfare Centre, he was always going in and out, but always had contact with the Phöinix staff " (JA Mrs. K. 35-37)

The first contact between André and the Care Workers happened at the Youth Welfare Office.

"Yeah an' that is how I got to know Werner. I was told: be here, let's say Wednesday at two o'clock at the Youth Welfare Office site "(André 127-129)."Well, then Werner was there, suddenly and one, two … hhmm later Mrs O. joined us as well" (André 130-132).

2.5. Key Themes and goals of the support

2.5.1. Problematic social behaviour

The Youth Welfare Office stated at the outset that delinquency was an issue:

"It was difficult to find a service which was able and prepared to work with someone who exhibited delinquent and criminal behaviour which also endangered him. Besides Phöinix e.V., very few institutions were prepared to help." (JA Mrs. K. 55-58)

Case notes testified that André exhibited both delinquent and violent behaviour. The same notes also mentioned concerns about prostitution but there was no evidence of this whilst André was cared for by "Jugendhilfe Phöinix e. V." and therefore the matter wasn't pursued further.

André described himself as criminal: *"An' I always had such a 'fuck it' attitude, I couldn't be bothered, I'd rather do illegal things" (André 50-51).*

The Youth Welfare Office confirmed this: *"André was always a strikingly aggressive teenager" (JA Mrs. K. 26).*

The Care Worker put it this way: *"Our main goal with Andre was to prevent him getting even worse ... because, at that time he was so antisocial anyway" (BE Werner M. 237-239).*

However André's delinquent behaviour continued to increase during the intervention and led to very dangerous situations for both himself and others:

> *"I mean André carried out one criminal action after another" (KO Mr. T. 72-73).* *"He attacked people with knives and I had to smash him against the wall" (BE Werner M. 255-256).* *"He was really life-threatening, throwing stones at an ICE* [rem: German express train] *and fire extinguishers at underground trains (S-Bahn)." (BE Werner M. 351-354).*

2.5.2. Emotional maturity

André's mother died of cancer in 1994, when he was 5 years old. His father was deeply moved as he told us that André did not know his mother: *"[...] he can't remember anything about his mother. Even when we visited the cemetery, he had no idea who lay there "(KV Mr. R. 399-400).*

The father says that André blamed him for his Mother's death: *"[...] he has always kept telling me that I am a shitty father, that it was my fault that he had no mother and so on" (KV Mr. R . 396-398).*

He described the everyday stress they experienced as a result of the loss. He said that there had been no help for them during the period of grieving immediately after his wife's death:

> *"We received no help at all in really. What there was were – how do you say it - 'grief seminars' to help you cope with the whole situation. But we were supposed to pay 4,000 Euros for them [unintelligible]. I didn't need a grief seminar, I say that you will never forget the mother or wife; you always carry her in your heart. And my par-*

ents in law didn't help with anything with regards to the kids. Not even for Birthdays, the kids' birthdays, Christmas, St Martin, anything."(KV Mr. R. 418-425).

The central theme for the father, that he was overwhelmed after the death of his wife became enmeshed with André and his brother's loss of their mother. Hence, there were two factors which had a major impact on the remaining family members: For once, the loss of a parent and secondly, the fact that there was no opportunity to go through a grieving process.

The caseworker at the Youth Welfare Office described André as: *"completely unable to develop relationships because he had never come to terms with the death of his mother. (JA Mrs. K. 316-317).*
"His trauma with his mother and her untimely death" (BE Werner M. 75-76) were themes which André pushed away and refused to discuss: *"[...] his mother was always a taboo with him he never really talked about it "*(BE Werner M. 535-536).

2.5.3. Family relationships

The first application for help was made to the Youth Welfare Office in June 2003 by his father who lived alone with André and was separated from his partner:

> "I lived <u>alone</u> with him, I lived with him <u>alone</u>. Later, I did have a relationship but my girlfriend couldn't take it. She said 'listen, this is... [rem: trails off mid-sentence] when we were on holiday or away he just caused havoc, drama without end. She said that her own children were grown up and she had enough of it. That's <u>partly</u> why the relationship broke down"(KV Mr. R. 125-130).

The pressures on his father made him turn away from André:

"I just couldn't do it any more, I didn't care, I wouldn't have believed that you wouldn't care about your kid anymore, I was a nervous wreck. At work, I always had to make sure that I finished work on time, get home quickly, and feed the kid and, and, and... it was a difficult situation for me "(KV Mr. R. 114-120).

He no longer collected André when he was picked up by police, he didn't have the strength or the will to help André whenever he had screwed up. *"I [rem: laughs] was totally overwhelmed with the boy, you can believe me" (KV Mr. R. 263-264).*
According to the case file the father was attested by a psychiatrist as being negligent in the care of his children and the stress experienced by André had an impact on his emotional development. The Care Worker said: *"He was just a street kid in the broadest sense of the word" (BE Werner M. 236-237). "And he never had a bond with his father who never had a positive role as a carer" (BE Werner M. 554-556).*

André confirmed that he had a very bad relationship with his father. His father hated him, but today he concedes that he had a right to: *"and rightly so, I'd say, it wasn't good for him when I messed up, and I didn't care "(André 281-285).*
The Care Worker also reports that the father favoured André's older brother Alex who was the *"Super Kid"*, and *"favourite son"*. André became the *"non-child" (BE Werner M. 191-198).*

The older brother allowed André to stay with him sometimes because *"he was, like, a bit the older brother ... but there was always jealousy, because the older brother had always got everything, you know, and the mother died so early" (BE Werner M. 211-214).*
In addition to the ambivalent relationship between the brothers
"There was still the father's girlfriend who tried to exercise the role of mother but was herself emotionally unstable. In her eyes, André was the completely asocial

son who she didn't want anything to do with. On other occasions, though, she'd make him offers along the lines of 'Come with me to Italy, I'll pay for your holiday' ... One day she'd fight with the father, the next day she'd play the caring mother. She became more the caring mother but that only really started after her relationship with his father ended. Since then she has been looking after his son"(BE Werner M. 211-220).

To summarise, André had no reliable place in this patchwork of confrontations, separations, jealousy and broken family relationships.

2.5.4. Life skills

André left school at 16 with no qualification which prevented him from developing any educational ambitions. After this he lived more or less on the street and survived from day to day.

Goals

Since no institution was willing to offer him a place anymore, the Youth Welfare Office decided to install a low intensity outpatient care which had, as its aim, to develop a relationship with André and influence him to achieve a gradual return to normality. *"So André is protected and that we would at least try to develop a relationship and persuade him to bring his behaviour back within acceptable limits"* (JA Mrs. K. 60-62).

Andrés own objectives were consistent with this aim. *"He had his own goals in mind at that time, he wanted to live alone and, and ... family, independence and away from his Father and getting away"* (BE Werner M. 85-87).

Case notes include further goals including:

- Accept boundaries without introducing rigid rules
- Accept consequences
- Community service in order to avoid the threatened imprisonment
- Contacts with parents, Supervised father-son contact with the aim of making the family system more robust and developing connections with André
- Future prospects (school, work)
- Regulatory support after the age of 18
- Clarify living situation (own home)

2.6. Resources of the young person and the family

2.6.1. André's resources

The Care Worker observed that André had many survival strategies:

"He has a native shrewdness, or so you could say. He has an instinct for survival" (BE Werner M. 122-123).

"He's always managed, he's always had something to eat, some money, from somewhere, he's always found a way" (BE Werner M. 146-148).

M. Werner also spoke of André's skill in using the system: *"He always gets by again and again, somehow, and tricking the system, he's learnt that well" (BE Werner M. 151-152).* In addition, André had a high degree of empathy: *"He's got a good feeling for who means well, who is being honest and who just wants to use him" (BE Werner M. 164-166).*

The Youth Welfare Office assessed André as capable of forming relationships, which was taken into account by the Care Worker. Both the Youth Welfare Office and the service co-ordinator described André to be 'charming and cute': *"So, he had charming and nice way with him that you couldn't be angry with him for long"* (KO Mr. T. 110-111). As a result, many doors were opened for André again and again.

2.6.2. Family resources

At the beginning of the intervention André's father could not provide any helpful resources:
> *"He was always happy to delegate all responsibility"* (BE Werner M. 178-179).
> *"The one resource in the family that could have been there for André to use, his father, was never available because he always sent André away"* (BE Werner M. 184-185).

This view is shared by the Youth Welfare Office, *"Yes, what resources? The father had absolutely none."*(JA Mrs. K. 148-149. The fact that the father was not able to fulfil his role as carer is mentioned many times: *"The father couldn't carry out his role as father"* (JA Mrs. K. 65-66), *"He didn't give a shit, always saying I don't give a shit even if he is my son. I'm not interested in what they do with him "*(BE Werner M. 567-568)*"And he's never had a bond with his father, actually, the father was never a really positive role model"* (BE Werner M. 554-556).

On the other hand the youth welfare officer describes the father as being very open and cooperative at times: *"the father is very open with me"* (JA Mrs. K. 388-389). At least, the father cannot be said to have obstructed support services.

2.7. Setting design

After the failure of the residential youth welfare measure, the multi-disciplinary team agreed that the only possible service would be a lower level of supervision but with intense outpatient support. "André was offered sleeping accommodation in a hotel *"because even the smallest requests led to confrontations – that's why we recommended an approach with a lower level of supervision in a hotel." (KO Mr. T. 29-30)* There were also objections:

> "On the other hand, and especially at night as well as weekends, there was a lack of control and lack of influence. In the end that's when the most difficult situations happened. The Youth Welfare Office knew that and it [rem: having him live in a hotel] was mostly because there was a lack of alternatives "(KO Mr. T. 31-34).

A high Care Worker ratio was approved to provide a dense mesh of support to limit André's criminal activities and damage: *"The main aim was to keep him off the streets "(BE Werner M. 282-283).*

Male and female Care Workers (both social workers) worked to provide André with experience of both parental roles. As a result of the high level of care giving André was introduced and integrated into the private life of the Care Workers. These included weekend activities and short holidays. These enabled the workers to develop a relationship to André as well as removing him from the street Milieu.

2.8. Participation of the young person and his parents

2.8.1. Participation of André

André could not understand the decision to provide outpatient care. Looking back in an interview, he said that, at the time, he was too immature: *"No, because I was basically too stupid back then to understand. Not mature enough. I thought, yo, this is a game"* (André 143-144).

He didn't agree with many of the decisions made and wasn't motivated to work on his future: *"So that was very, very stressful for me, because Werner, Ulrike was there and then Mrs K, and they decided some things which I didn't agree with, and that's when I usually I went berko"* (André 253-255).

In Contrast, the Care Worker viewed the decision making process as fully involving André *"so it was clear it was clear to him that he wanted to get away from his father but needed someone to help to accompany him, he already had his own goals in his mind"* (BE Werner M. 83-85). This coincides with a review of the Youth Welfare Officer: *"I think he realised fairly quickly that he had to accept help if he wasn't going to slip further down"* (JA Mrs. K. 97-99).

In the end the multidisciplinary team listened to the message that André had sent through being repeatedly thrown out of residential care and, despite the risks and dangers posed by him, cared for him on the street and in the hotel without any further inpatient residential placements.

2.8.2. Participation of parents

The father made an application for help with care and education because he couldn't manage André anymore. The father took no further part in the subsequent planning of care and support.

"The Father didn't feel that this decision was unusual, to him it was just a relief that he was finally rid of the responsibility" (JA Mrs. K. 92-94). The father remembers it in a similar way: "*I pretty much signed everything without looking at it; they said they only needed a signature*" (KV Mr. R. 158-159).

However he regularly took part in the discussions with the Youth Welfare Officers and in the discussions with the Care Workers: "*Yeah, well, we've had some talks, there was always some kind of meeting, like with the Youth Welfare Office,*" (KV Mr. R. 345-346).

"*So I tried to do as best I could what the Youth Welfare Office wanted me to do*" (KV Mr. R. 330-331).

2.9. The Quality of the relationship between the young person and the support services

2.9.1. André – Care Workers M. Werner and Ulrike O.

André describes the relationship both to Werner M. as well as to Ulrike O. as very good:

"*That Werner, he, he is a very, very good Care Worker. I'd say, whoever has him* [rem: as Care Worker] *is going to be happy with him.*" (André 71-73).

"*There was Ulrike ... really nice for me, really all right*" (André 165-166).

"*And as it was, it was a very good relationship*" (André 196).

"*We won't go our separate ways, definitely not*" (André 204).

To date, there is still contact between Werner M. and André, which is initiated by André. Werner M. refers to the relationship with André as trusting and good: "*It was relatively clear that the chemistry was right" (BE Werner M. 64-65).* Werner M. became a kind of father figure:

> *"So I was André's father for four years, literally" (BE Werner M. 186-187).*
>
> *"As the relationship was clear and became more robust and then, almost naturally, there were these small changes in him" (BE Werner M. 265-267).*
>
> *"He trusted me, I was very authentic" (BE Werner M. 268).*

This relationship was characterised by both honesty and consistency *"So if I committed to anything, then I stuck to it" (BE Werner M. 363-364).* The focus was on the relationship and intimacy:

> *"And I believe that exactly this great closeness, that was the great opportunity for this process, I think" (BE Werner M. 449-450).*
>
> *"When I look back three years there's a lot, a lot's happened. I don't think that it would have happened if it had not been for the relationship that we've had over the last four years "(BE Werner M. 460-462).*

This assessment is also supported by the Youth Welfare Office:

> *"It was clear pretty quickly that André had developed a bond with both Care Workers" (JA Mrs. K. 71-72).*
>
> *"Everything seemed to fit and therefore André was able to open himself relatively quickly and could accept help." (JA Mrs. K. 104-105)*
>
> *"And if someone had any influence, it was clearly the Care Workers" (JA Mrs. K. 127).*

The coordinator also confirmed that there was a good relationship between André and his Care Workers which helped prevent the situation from getting worse: *"So, it was good for him to have some stable relationships" (KO Mr. T. 93).* Furthermore it was stressed that the Care Worker was always there for André as someone to rely on, regardless of whatever happened before.

> *"André always came back and returned again and again. He knew exactly that Werner M. was there for him." (KO Mr. T. 200-201).*
> *"One had just accepted André as he was and didn't question it as much." (KO Mr. T. 216-217).*

The father also acknowledged the existence of the bond between André and Werner M.: *"And… somehow Mr M. managed to develop a connection to him" (KV Mr. R. 259-260).*

2.10. Process design between young person and the support services

2.10.1. Social behaviour

The Care Worker worked a lot with boundaries, made sure André toed the line and showed him the consequences of his behaviour:

> *"Yes, so, to begin with it was all about constantly setting limits with André. To develop a system where when I say something you do it and I am the adult and you are still just about an adolescent and we don't have discussions, I decide for you and that's it."(BE Werner M. 244-249).*
> *"I think that this is a sort of confrontational clarity" (BE Werner M. 103).*

Hence, if André did not adjust his behaviour adequately, the Care Worker withdrew.

> "So really, you don't do this to me, when you start with your antisocial comments like Adolf and so on then I'll go or put the phone down or then you won't see me again today" (BE Werner M . 239-251).
>
> "And that happening to him in puberty [laughs]... that's a massive challenge to have to experience those limits, physically as well. I sat on him and wrapped myself around him "(BE Werner M. 253-255).
>
> "[rem: It was necessary] to manage to set boundaries, to show him clear boundaries in puberty" (BE Werner M. 320-321).

Boundaries, confronting, immediacy, authenticity and endurance were keywords in the support programme.

> "The most useful interventions were when I really grabbed André, when I held onto him or even smashed him against the wall. Like that time when he suddenly attacked somebody with two knives and I just gripped him and said you won't be stabbing anybody as long as I stand next to you." (BE Werner M. 406-410)

There were always a lot of talks on the topics of delinquency, aggression and values: *"There was repeated conflict, I believe it was these conflicts that prevented other things happening"* (BE Werner M. 310- 311). It was important on one side to set boundaries but on the other to make it possible for him to see that he was always welcome when he thought about his behaviour and sought to change it. *"I think it was just this clear stop, stop, it doesn't work like this – here is the boundary and I like you anyway."*(BE Werner M. 107-108)

André stressed that M. Werner supported him with problems at any time: *"If you have a problem, then he sorts it out with you, immediately"* (André 65). André highlighted the often de-escalating behaviour of the Care Worker: *"When there are times of stress, stay calm, don't get your knickers in a twist, and don't always freak out. He taught me that"(André 88-89)*. The Care Worker always left a door open and this was described by the coordinator in the following way:

> *"I did notice that sometimes he swore at Mr M. but he always came back again and again and he always knew that Werner M. was there for him and that Werner never took things personally"(KO Mr. T. 198-202).*
>
> *"One day he was yelling, carrying on like a pork chop... then Werner sent him away and said: When you've calmed down again, you know where to find me"(KO Mr. T. 205, 207-208).*

To be straightforward with youths can be said to be one of the important interventions.

> *"Werner M. is really able to speak the same language as André, he could deal with it very well. He wasn't too intellectual or behaved like a teacher and wasn't preachy, he spoke simple and was clear about what he meant"(KO Mr. T. 156-159).*

The Coordinator emphasises the legal work carried out by the Care Worker for André.

"He really stood up for André's rights; it was good that André had his rights protected. Werner M made sure that he did" (KO Mr. T. 193-194). In summary, the role consisted mainly of accepting him:

> *"And it was such a constant up and down because nobody could put up with André" (BE Werner M. 285-286).*
>
> *"And of course having to put up with his emotional attacks and his antisocial behaviour required a lot of endurance and stamina "(Werner M. 397-399).*
>
> *"He trusted me because I was very authentic" (BE Werner M. 268).*

The Youth Welfare Office also considered the following intervention strategy to be very valuable *"The almost constant availability of the male Care Worker was... very helpful"* (JA Mrs. K. 209-210). This was confirmed by the coordinator:

> *"This intensive support and responsiveness was a significant and specific help and was possible as a result of the number of hours available. He was able to contact the Care Workers on a daily basis"* (KO Mr. T. 88-90).

2.10.2. Emotional maturity

It is unfortunate that there were few opportunities offered to André to retrospectively complete his grieving process. The interviews only contain the already quoted evidence of how André rejected the subject as taboo:

> *"Whew. That was <u>never</u> brought into discussions because any attempt to work on grieving such as saying farewell, visiting to the cemetery or to discuss it was always rejected by André."* (BE Werner M. 527-529)

This raises the question as to what degree those supporting André were themselves 'infected' by the taboo.

The theme of personal development and maturing led to a range of interventions beginning with the design of the setting with a man and a woman as Care Workers.

> *"And then we had the idea to bring a female colleague into play, so that Andre can work on his relationships to females again"* (BE Werner M. 530-531).
>
> *"For a while there was a female colleague, in part addressing the trauma caused by his mother's untimely*

death, so to that we could cover this role "(BE Werner M. 271-273).

"However, Ulrike O took on a completely different role, partly level headed and partly loving. I would not say that Werner M. was not loving, but just in a different way. She mothered him a bit, went clothes shopping with him, cooked a bit for him and looked after him in a different way. I found it was actually lovely... a beautiful connection. So, that was a nice combination"(KO Mr. T. 165-171).

"The female Care Worker... had a motherly nature, she could take André in her arms, she cooked with him on the weekend and invited him to come round, or baked cakes, so just like a mother, a very warm-hearted being and that was exactly right "(JA Mrs. K. 119-123).

However, as a result of the different approaches of the two Care Workers this approach was cancelled after one year. The coordinator made the following interesting interpretation:

"As an outsider you could almost say that they became André's father and mother, it was almost a transference. As such it was a reflection of the system [...] with occasional arrangements and agreements and also revealing the phenomenon of what had happened. We tried to get them to arrive at a common denominator, but it didn't work, I think that some of André's story was projected on to the Care Worker or it was a repeat "(KO Mr. T. 180-191).

The father's girlfriend was also able to partially fill the role of mother.

> *"His father's girlfriend took on a bit of a mother's role dependent on how she felt, what sort of stress she was having with the father. She fulfilled the role of a provider to some extent but did not meet André's emotional needs" (BE Werner M. 537-539).*

As a "highlight" in the care process, the Care Worker describes an intervention with André that was likely to have given him the opportunity to catch up on some of his childhood:

> *"I carried out a sort of delayed childhood with André. I said once to him that if he behaved like that again I'd buy him a baby's dummy and this 16-year old really wanted one, and then we went to his football club because it had to be one of his team's and I bought one and he wore it for three months day and night, in the middle of the city, on the street, flirted with girls with it, but he carried on wearing this baby's dummy and then we spent a week playing in a sandpit and after that, the subject was finished. That's how he became a young man.. I think it had something to do with the need to express his pent up feelings about his mother although she was never mentioned."(BE Werner M. 545-554).*

2.10.3. Family relationships

When the support began there was no contact between father and son. *"Over time he began to make contact with his son through the Care Worker, the male Care Worker" (JA Mrs. K. 147-148).* First, the Care Worker had the task to de-escalate the conflict between father and son when they were direct contact. The father remembers his first meeting with the Care Worker Werner M.:

"Werner M., I first met him when we had such conflict at home ... or ... I don't know any more, and as I said, one word led to the other. André said something to me and I wanted to give him a good hiding. Mr. Werner was there and he tried to calm the situation down"(KV Mr. R. 102-105).

"It was always difficult to arrange any contact when André wanted to see his father ... and then only with bullying and insulting" (BE Werner M. 198-200). In the later stages of the care programme it became even possible for the three of them to have a day out together. It is interesting that the father felt that this was possible because André had improved.

"And later when things got better, we went to McDonalds or met for Father's Day, at a football match on Father's Day or whatever, you were there, too."(KV Mr. R. 109-113).

The coordinator suspected the father was "an issue with André every day":

"I can remember that André was talking about his father, even if he met him briefly at McDonalds, or ringing him again and asking for money. We found it difficult to get the father involved."(KO Mr. T. 285-290)

He also remembered that the two brothers and the father were always in contact – even if it was only about their disputes:

"So, although there was still the other brother and although each of them complained about the other... and from the outside it looked like they were arguing with each other every day, they were still in touch with each other; even if it was only to argue. I reckon that was of some use. There was never a time when one or *the other broke off the relationship. The father did complain a lot about André and André about his father and then the other brother about the father and André. Despite all of this the family still held ... and they were also there for each other. Mr R. also maintained contact with Werner M. and was in dialogue and - I believe tried to offer André something within the realm of his abilities but met his limits."(KO Mr. T. 295-307).*

As the end of the programme came closer,
"Suddenly, the father went into provider mode, saying 'if you come to my place, I'll cook for you'. He used to do that every now and again but then André came half an hour too late and he [rem: the dad] *had thrown the food in the rubbish bin and then there was rampage and arguments and then nothing for months and then just as I withdrew or it was clear that I was withdrawing, then he started arguing with me. Increasingly, as the end of the programme drew near the father began competing with me. In the last months of the programme he was trying to win André over which led of course to a complete conflict for André because Werner was going and a new person was coming and he was sort of fighting for me and said that suddenly Werner was shit "*(BE Werner M. 571-583).

The way André dealt with the issue of the competition between his two "fathers" (biological father and the Care Worker) by rejecting the Care Worker made it easier for André to leave the programme. As to what degree this process supported his acceptance by his family remains unclear.

The Case Worker from the Youth Welfare Office recognised how hard the Care Workers worked to get André's father involved with his son but she pointed out the rivalry between Care Worker and Father:

"Phöinix worked with what was possible with regard to the cooperation and involvement of the father, he's always tried to involve the father, Werner M. has. On the other hand I've already described the difficulties arising out of the rivalry between Father and Care Worker. Within the intellectual limits, the father is limited too; naturally you shouldn't forget that, Phöinix did well in the field of parent cooperation. They made an effort to reason with the father and try to get him to get closer and to think about what it means to be a father but as I said you must always regard the limits of the father."(JA Mrs. K. 278-287)

André wasn't able to develop a relationship with the father's girlfriend during the course of the programme although she made contact with the father again as the programme came to an end. The Care Worker said that the relationship was mixed, sometimes she was there and sometimes not dependent on how her relationship with the father was going. (cf. BE Werner M. 537-539.)

"They had ended their relationship and he had moved out as I said at the beginning and she wasn't prepared to work with Phöinix. She didn't want anything to do with André."(JA Mrs. K. 287-292)

2.10.4. Life skills

André went through a variety of accommodations during the programme including a hotel, the street, staying with friends, at a campsite and in shelters. He had to move again and again because of his behaviour. The Coordinator assessed it in the following way: *"In retrospect perhaps André relied too much on the support and risked more and more because he thought that the support would always get him out of trouble"(KO Mr. T. 390-393)*.

The development of educational career prospects similarly suffered, his other problems overshadowing them which is why these topics were not mentioned in any of the interviews and what, if any, progress he was making.

2.11. Stakeholder collaboration

Communication between the Co-ordination and Care Workers was sometimes difficult because there were two Care Workers: "Ulrike O. would say that she would have liked to have had more support from Phöinix" (KO Mr. T. 242-243). When the number of Care Workers was reduced to one, the communication was much better: "The Coordinator felt much closer even to André and better informed about the issues [...] I would really say since then co-operation has gone well" (KO Mr. T. 245-246, 248).

The Care Worker explained that Phöinix eV at the time still operated almost like a family business. Everybody knew everybody else and that in turn produced a climate of trust and furthered cooperation: *"They were just a very supportive organisation because they knew you very well, so they were pretty much on the ball with everything you were doing."(BE Werner M. 485-487).* At the same time the Care Worker also saw the dangers of running the business like that:

> *"It takes the possibilities of confrontation away or objective reflection so you can avoid hurting the other" (BE Werner M. 479-481).*
>
> *"If this nice friendly Goochy Goo approach breaks down - then everything becomes more professional and structured ... I could call Mr. T. at ten at night and say, I just have to talk about the case, which was completely okay "(BE Werner M. 514-517).*

The Coordinator felt that the Communication and cooperation with the Youth Welfare Office was very difficult and not very supportive as a result of the repeated failures of earlier attempts to work with the family.

> *"The difficulties of communication with the Youth Welfare Office were a particular issue, the case worker was overworked and overwhelmed with the work in general but in particular with André " (KO Mr. T. 66-69).*
> *"The cooperation with the Youth Welfare Office, I would really say that's not gone well" (KO Mr. T. 336-337).*

The Coordinator is critical of the Youth Welfare Office in that they transferred all responsibility to the outpatient care service, whilst at the same time being rather demanding by making daily calls and asking for information, *"Sometimes the Youth Welfare Office overstepped its bounds" (KO Mr. T. 356-357).*

A very different assessment is made by the Youth Welfare Office. They experienced the communication and cooperation with the service provider and with the Care Workers as very positive, *"I can only say that the cooperation has been very positive" (JA Mrs. K. 247).* *"We had regular bi-monthly contact with the Care Workers ... and if there was something very urgent we immediately made contact" (JA Mrs. K. 249-252).* There was also good co-operation with other stakeholders such as the hotel manager which the Coordinator evaluated as positive.

> *"The Care Worker worked well with the manager of the hotel. For example, the ambulant Care Workers, well, Werner M. collaborated with the hotel manager. ... This worked very well, Werner M was always well informed on time and the other way round "(KO Mr. T. 363-366).*

2.12. Conclusion of the programme and ongoing support

Although he wasn't yet able to live independently and responsibly at the age of 18, the programme was terminated early because of the lack of involvement by André.

Departure

The termination of the programme was announced at an early stage but all of the participants felt like having been thrown in at the deep end: *"And I'd say this is very, very hard when you no longer have the support, because then you have to fight alone" (André 421-422)* but André has also taken it as an opportunity to wake up and do something.

> *"So luckily I recognized very early .., so these few yards I have just woken up and thought: Oh, the programme is over now and I just have to take as much as I can, and then I just joined in with them ... So it helped "(André 422-425).*

The Care Worker sees the termination of the programme as being deficient:

> *"In my opinion, I don't think that the preparation for transition was done well by the Youth Welfare Office" (BE Werner M. 648-649).*
>
> *"They didn't make any preparations they just said we are closing down, we finish up, we will only provide legal assistance on" (BE Werner M. 656-657).*
>
> *"I didn't even say goodbye to him properly, me not to him and him not to me"(BE Werner M. 690-691).*

This statement is based on the background that the Care Worker still supports André on a voluntary basis. *"I believe he is one of those guys, yes ... yes there's no goodbye because somehow there is still a relationship"* (BE Werner M. 701-702). Continued support is provided through a legal representative.

> *"André is now an adult but his intellectual limitations mean that I have made an application for statutory legal support so that he has someone who can help him in further applications for help from social services or housing and protects his rights"*(JA Mrs. K. 298-302).

There was no further support for André except the voluntary support of his ex-Care Worker. The following facts are based on what happened after the end of the programme.

André had his own flat and legal support. Apart from this, he had no educational or career options, lived from social welfare money and is more or less still involved in criminal activities. Those involved in his support are sceptical of the prognosis for his future life. *"As the programme came to an end we didn't have the slightest idea whether he would manage"* (BE Werner M. 719-720). *"I've always known that when the programme comes to an end it'd be only a question of time before he ends up in prison"* (KO Mr. T. 389-390).

The Youth Welfare Office saw the completion of the programme in a slightly more positive way: *"I was satisfied with the programme and even after. Let me tell you I have got some other cases I could say a thing or two about them. But I was satisfied with the outcome for André because he was a really one of the most difficult cases"* (JA Mrs. K. 334-337).

2.13. The impact of the support and its effects as seen by the interviewees

2.13.1. Social behaviour

André described himself as having learnt to be more respectful of other people as a result of the programme:

> "And Werner and, yeah he, yes he achieved a lot with me, I learnt a lot, how you get on with people, show them respect and so on" (André 69 -71).
> "And he said 'Yes even if there are times of stress, stay calm. Keep a low profile, don't always freak out like that'. So that is what Werner taught me." (André 88-89).

André showed fewer tendencies to commit criminal acts: *"Yeah, I reached a point where I didn't mess up as much anymore"* (André 242-243). Even though all of the people who had been involved in his support thought that he would end up in prison sooner or later when the programme finished, André managed to surprise them. *"In retrospective, more has happened than we were able to see and have seen"* (BE Werner M. 737-738).

André has a good grip on his tendency towards criminal and anti-social behaviour: *"He's learnt to approach conflicts more calmly and to avoid both verbal and physical aggression or violence against objects"* (JA Mrs. K. 319-320).

2.13.2. Emotional Maturity

André's emotional development has stabilised, *"I think he has managed to trust at least one adult – without exploiting him"* (BE Werner M. 759-760). *"He understands that relationships have an intrinsic worth over and above just using them as a way of surviving"* (BE Werner M. 766-767). The Youth Welfare Office sees the improvement in emotional maturity as of being of particular importance: *"under the guidance of Phöinix there has been a leap in his emotional maturity"* (JA Mrs. K. 314-315).

2.13.3. Family relationships

André feels that he has a very positive relationship with his father now: *"Well, my father and I, we now have a super relationship"* (André 269). *"They helped us get together, the relationship between me and my father is better"* (André 276-277).

At the end of the programme the Care Worker noticed positive changes in the father-son relationship, which had been hitherto characterised by constant outbursts of emotion, conflicts and recurring breakups. The amount of family conflicts has been reduced and the father has taken responsibility at the end of the programme:

> *"Ahh .. for the first time the father discovered what he is able to do – or at least rediscovered what he's capable of doing in the care for his son when my care stopped"* (BE Werner M. 188-190).

> *"The, phh, the connection became a successful one when I withdrew from providing care"* (BE Werner M. 561-562).

> *"But nowadays I think he spends nearly every day, somehow, with his father"* (BE Werner M. 591-592).

2.13.4. Life skills

André only 'woke up' when the programme finished:
> *"So some people only wake up later, maybe at seventeen, eighteen. Woke up a bit then and thought, oh, [chuckles] the Youth Welfare services will finish soon...*

> *Then I'll have to do something, yeah, and then the hotel said they had a job, yeah. ... 'You can start here, we'll give it a go' and now everything's working out"(André 51-55).*
>
> *"In the past when I had to pay bills or something like that, he showed me how to do it - you should pay for it immediately and not leave it for three weeks, four or six weeks of course I'm a bit like that and now if anything comes, I pay it immediately "(André 84-87).*

His attitude towards work and money has also changed. He found a permanent part-time job in the hotel where he has been living for much of the programme *"He was even hired as a receptionist two years ago" (BE Werner M. 263-264).*

> *"I want to go to work; it makes a better impression, especially with the girls" (André 450-451).*
>
> *"What's the state doing with the money that bone idle people like this – they can't be bothered to do anything and I thought, hmm I have to find a way. If other people can do it then I can do it, too. "(André 455-456).*
>
> *"I'm having fun and now I know how it feels when you do something and can afford a few things" (André 463-464).*

André now lives in his own apartment with a long term rental agreement and has regular employment although he still hasn't completed his high school qualification.

> *"What else was there, ah yeah, in his own flat, that went relatively well and he had his own space at last" (BE Werner M. 287-288).*
>
> *"So he always kept his apartment clean and tidy, he did really well, he even managed to stay in his last flat until last year" (BE Werner M. 298-300).*

"He managed to sign a rental contract by himself. He organised the move through ARGE and all this other stuff, he's got his own bank account that he controls, it all works " (BE Werner M. 720-724).

The co-ordinator recognises that the things André learnt through the programme could only be put into practice when the programme finished: *"But otherwise I saw a chance for André" (KO Mr. T. 439-440).* His father also sees positive changes in André, *"I would say he is good, more self-confident, more responsible, and more independent" (KV Mr. R. 432-433).* At the same time he mentions that André also has very unrealistic plans for the future: *"He wants to be a professional football player" (KV Mr. R. 445-446).*

2.14. André's ideas for his future

André made some plans: *"Well ... Now I would definitely like to finish school." (André 490-491). "And when I start school again, I'd also like to get my driver's license." (André 496)*

2.15. Summary

When the work with André finished at the end of the programme, the prognosis for his future life was not positive. A superficial inspection of the case notes described repeated violence, criminality and the refusal of any offers of help to move forwards into the future. A prison term appeared to be the most likely outcome when the programme finished. This was the unanimous opinion.

The reconstructive view, however, received unexpected justification through a surprise about turn in André's life. The basis of this was the deepness of the relationship between André and his Care Worker and the latter's persistence and patience which leads to the conclusion that André was able to use these experiences for personal development much more than was apparent at the end of the programme.

It is noteworthy that the Carer always managed to hang on to André and stay with him. He was able to differentiate between André as a person and his actions. The Care Worker never tolerated violent or criminal behaviour and always drew consistent consequences both in word and action. Despite the delinquent behaviour, Werner was always able to welcome and include André. This appears to be a particular characteristic of this programme that André was able to internalise changes in his own behaviour and was able to use these behaviours and skills in his independent life. It required the Care Worker to be able to reflect honestly on his work as well as a high level of persistence and engagement well beyond the call of duty.

An additional important aspect which has contributed to André's relative stability is that the Care Worker has maintained contact and supported him occasionally with meetings or other formalities after the Youth Welfare Office programme ended.

Some issues that were considered important were not dealt with due to many uncertainties during the programme such as the disagreements between the Care Workers which led to a need to deal with further leavetaking and the lack of the opportunity to grieve. Despite this, or luckily, these weaknesses have not stood in the way of a positive development for André.

3. Case Study Christian

Sources:
- File analysis
- Interviews with:
    - Christian (the Young Person)
    - Care Worker in Germany (BE Heike A.)
    - Care Worker in Italy (BE Klaus B.)
    - Coordinator (KO Mr S.)
    - Care Worker's partner in Germany (U)

3.1. Current situation

The interview was held with Christian in a small hotel in L. The interviewer met a stocky young man who was big and strong but not particularly sporty. He was dressed in black and the interviewer noticed he wore a black coat – even though it was the end of June and warm outside

At the time of the interview Christian was 26 years old and lived in his own small flat in L. He was an apprentice silversmith and was repeating his third year as a result of too many absences.

The young man described himself as having a relatively large circle of friends. He didn't have any particular hobbies. He described his recreational activities as follows:

"On the weekends [laughs] we drink a lot of alcohol, er, really, er, sitting together, talking, and watching films and play computer games. Sometimes we go around the countryside here in the woods, it's very attractive. I've, er, often gone for a walk with my friends, had picnics, so quite bourgeois really [clears his throat]" (Christian 20-24)

3.2. Case history

Sources: case files, interviews

Start of treatment:	1999
Age at entry:	15
Termination of support:	31.06.2003
Duration of the Programme:	ca 4 years

Care Notes

1999 to February 2001
Cared for by Care Worker Heike A. in a supported living group (SLG) for 1.5 years, expelled for regularly breaking the rules, several months on the street while existing Carer Worker continued to work with him

April 2001 to July 2002
Residential 1:1 care in a residential project in Italy, cared for by Care Workers Klaus B and wife in a very rural and isolated place. Programme discontinued at Christian's choice when he became adult.

2nd July 2002 to 31st June 2006

Ambulant transitional care in own flat with reduced hours from the original Care Worker Heike A.

3.3. History

The files provided very little information about Christian's history. The only available information came from Christian himself and his Carer Workers during the interviews.

Christian said that prior to beginning with "Jugendhilfe Phöinix e. V." at the age of 15, he lived in an emergency shelter and youth accommodation and remembered the incidents which led to his rejection from his family home:

> "because, as far as I can remember I didn't do anything except push my mother away during this argument, ehrm, but the next day she threw me out, so I had to pack my stuff somehow and go, her and her boyfriend at the time, left me in this emergency shelter in L., ehrm, I was thrown out of school at the same time" (Christian 117-122).

His later Care Worker Heike A. talked of Christian experiencing a violent inner conflict as a result of being thrown out:

> "because he was incredibly confused, because he was away from his mother, it just got worse at home, really bad and [...] But I think a bit hurt and resentful at the same time that he couldn't stay at home, although he didn't want to anyway ..." (BE Heike A 35-38).

The Care Worker in Italy – Klaus B. talked about the problem of having so little information about Christian right at the beginning of the interview:

> *"I have to say that I didn't know much about Christian's history. I didn't get many records that I could have used to prepare at the time. From my point of view that would have been desirable at the time, to have known more, family background and the reasons specific decisions had been made" (BE Klaus B. 40-42).*

But Klaus was certain that "he had had a lot of negative experiences in his family which led to him behave in a way that was neither of benefit to him nor society." (BE Klaus B. 40-42) He went on to say:

> *"Only that the young man was never listened to, that he was never trusted to experience anything intellectually, physically or vocationally. He was never allowed... I think, to express himself. I don't think that his parents and others were able to cope with him, he was just a lot more intelligent than many other people"* (BE Klaus B. 104-108).

In 1999, the Youth Welfare Office referred Christian to a newly founded supported living group (SLG) for young people run by "Jugendhilfe Phöinix e. V."

In the few "relatively vague reports" available, Christian was described as being *"capable of living in a group to a limited extent"* (KO Herr S. 31).

3.4. Initiating Contact / Initial Approach for Help

The Coordinator remembered the initial contact and referral:

> *"We had just opened a supported living group for youths in G. and had some capacity. The group was designed for a maximum of three young people and Christian was referred by the Youth Department of the city of L. for a residential stay. He was described as being able to live in a small group and was 'recommended' by a colleague Mrs P from L. for the SG. We decided to accept Christian after a brief period familiarisation and receiving the few reports"* (KO Herr S. 7-14).

Christian didn't seem to remember or wish to remember much about the beginning of the programme. It is possible that this showed how stressful he found this time to be.

> *"Ehrm, to be honest [...] I don't really remember much of what happened after I met Mr S in the emergency shelter, ah, if I remember rightly - after a few conversations that somehow I was taken to this youth support group in G., I'm not really sure now but I think that I met a Care Worker at the time [...]"* (Christian 70-75).

He didn't remember his experience in the supported living group as having been successful. He blames both the staff and the physical environment.

> *"Erhm, I'm pretty sure that I met Heike A first on the day I moved in. .. My first impressions weren't very positive, some-*

thing had happened [...] that... the Care Worker or a Supervisor at the time had somehow attempted suicide, that was [laughs] funny at first and then, ehrm, no idea, and of the house, of the house itself.. didn't make any positive impression because, it was somehow pretty much a hole, because the house was very old somehow, mmm" (Christian 94-103).

The Care Worker of the support group told how she came to work with Christian:

"[...] at the time I was contacted by a colleague in the emergency shelter who asked if I could imagine, ... working as a 1:1 Care Worker because [laughing] he really thought that I would be good at it. So I applied for the job and, ah, Christian was my first Young Person" (BE Heike A. 27-31).

3.5. Key themes and goals of the support

3.5.1. Problematic social behaviour

The Coordinator perceived an *"unpredictable disposition to violence"* during the first phase of the care programme (KO Mr S. 186).

The question of whether he was *"mentally ill or... pretending to be"* was contentious for the support services *"but even the psychiatrists were unable to answer it for a long time"* (KO Herr S. 187-188).

In one conversation on the telephone with Christians Therapist Dr Y (22.11.2000) said that Christian was a *"very sick young person"* he expressed the suspicion that Christian displayed narcissistic and depressive personality traits. However, the case file contained no psychiatric diagnosis.

The memories of the Care Worker suggest that Christian believed that everything that happened around him somehow had something to do with him. He felt that any questioning of his behaviour was an insult to his person.

The Care Workers described Christian as controlling and playing power games. Sometimes he was needy and sometimes threatening. He expressed phantasies about death and violence and had a solid philosophical knowledge of these subjects. At the same time he was unable to cope with everyday challenges arising out of living with other people. Christian enjoyed talking a lot but resisted acting, he had ignored rules or broken them and could not be persuaded otherwise (BE Heike A. 39-43).

The Care Worker described Christian as: *"actually a totally fearful personality"* (BE Heike A 81-82) which was obvious when it came to having new experiences (e.g. going to a Hunnen-Camp *[rem: outdoor camp, similar to the medieval markets]*, flying in airplanes and so on).

Many of the Care Workers felt threatened in their work with Christian:

> *"... was clear pretty quickly that I was his and only his Care Worker, his Heike .. anyway, none of the other young people were allowed with me, mmm,.. and at the same time he was consistently threatening me, consistently, extremely sexualised .. (showing me himself) naked as he opened the door, not wanting to get dressed, anyway lots of stuff that was very childish but naturally came over as a bit strong from a 15 year old young man"* (BE Heike A. 43-51)

"Yes, because he did, I was, there was a long phase [...] where I really only went in to the support group house with my back against the wall because he stood there with a knife, or he used to have a long sword . mm, .. I was always scared that something would go wrong, I mean situations where I'd come into the house and there is blood everywhere and that wouldn't have been very funny" (BE Heike A. 159-165)

The Care Worker in Italy felt that Christian suffered from the suspected personality disorders but he also observed things that had previously gone unnoticed:

"[...] I found contradictions in these basic assumptions, I told myself after my first conversation with Christian: there is something there, it's not a rigid, crusted over, static situation. The assumptions that have been made, these disturbances could... if... if they were now addressed, could be changed a bit or mitigated" (BE Klaus B. 132-137)

He remembered Christian as a very night loving person whose main subject was *"death and violence in its widest sense"* (BE Klaus B. 63). He was *"very pale [...] with an immobile face, hardly a muscle movement [...] hardly an eye movement and he was wearing a long, thick, black leather coat in the Italian spring sunshine that reminded one of the NS (Nazi) times in Germany or simply a dark power, Goethe's Faust or Shakespeare's Macbeth for example. A person who has decided to represent the darker side of humanity"* (BE Klaus B. 164-170).

However, the Care Worker and his colleagues managed, through being approachable and respectful to look past the threatening exterior:

> *"And he carried the whole thing like armour, when he peeled himself out of his layers of clothes there stood a handsome young man who looked more vulnerable than anything else.... but then he had painted himself black to give a particular picture of himself ... you can fuck off, you can't do anything to me, I'm just waiting my time up but you won't change me"* (BE Klaus B. 174-179).

He sketched a picture of Christian whose manner depended on his environment. He had developed interests and behaviour which *"gave him security from attack"*. His attempts at antagonising other people by confronting them with his thoughts on death, life after death, phantasies about death and violence served the purpose of showing the world: "listen up, this is my world, this is the world I live in..." On the other hand we quickly realised that he simply questioned this philosophy. At the time he listened to Death Metal bands, Black Metal bands, the hardest heavy metal, English and German bands that represented something satanic for him.

> *"And... we realised really quickly that he didn't have any other way of being in Germany. Behaving like this he would at least be taken seriously. It's obvious that somebody shaking a gravestone and casually talking about wanting to dig up bodies will cause people to pay attention. Or walking through the fair wearing outlandish clothes and carrying an axe or a sword*

over your shoulder will make sure somebody notices you!" (BE Klaus B. 198-203).

The Coordinator found Christian to be one of the *"most interesting and certainly most difficult young persons in the last 15 years [...] and in retrospect definitely on the boundary between psychiatry and youth welfare support [...]"* (KO Herr S. 302-305).

3.5.2. Emotional maturity

As Christian was referred to "Jugendhilfe Phöinix e. V." at the age of 15 he still had the emotional maturity of a small child. He wanted the Care Worker to take him to bed and have lullabies sung to him. He talked like a small complaining child, wanted to be held and comforted but was at the same time threatening. (BE Heike A. 46-51):

> *"Therefore Christian always used the tactic of behaving like a small child because his experience with his mother when he did that was that she had always given in. Therefore he spat his dummy over not getting a bar of chocolate in the supermarket to 'I'll kill you'"* (BE Heike A. 333-336).

The Care Worker in Italy noticed that the 17 year old Christian didn't have any experience of playing:

> *"Christian was a person who approached life in a very rational way. Rational but drifting off into phantasy, into an unreal world, because the real world wasn't absolutely his world. The*

more so because in his childhood he hadn't able to experience playing using his hands, to experience things, to work with them" (BE Klaus B. 314-317).

3.5.3. Family relationships

Not much is known about the family situation except that Christian was thrown out of the home because of physical violence towards his mother. He said in interviews that *"as a young person he never got on"* with his mother and accepts a certain degree of responsibility. *"That was because my mother mmm, was a very difficult person and, aah, I wasn't exactly wearing a halo and .. I didn't like school, refused to go to school"* (Christian 111-114).

The Care Worker in Italy told us that there were also two teenage daughters. He assumed that the mother was overwhelmed with caring for three children. She gave the impression of being frail and slightly esoteric and very concerned with herself. He felt that she was more emotionally cold than warm and that *"Christian was the black sheep of the family"* and that he, and certainly his family couldn't deal with it. (BE Klaus B. 117-119).

> *"I think that he was very strongly rejected before he came to us"* and further *"I think that his family and many others had categorised him as borderline psychopath. On the basis that he was somebody who would have to live for ever in a psychiatric hospital or something similar. He really suffered because it*

wasn't really true, he felt misunderstood" (BE Klaus B. 119-125)

Christian can remember a very difficult relationship with his mother:

"I would say that at the time I didn't have any relationship with my mother, we used to talk on the phone sometimes but, aah, I can remember that we used to argue a lot and then after every argument there was radio silence for a while" (Christian 204-207)

As far as the Care Worker could remember the mother also had a partner *"and he used to listen to music that Christian liked and he liked him but that sort of faded out"*. Despite the constant arguments, Christian always felt drawn to his mother *"he had always been rejected by the father figures. I think that that was a big point, which had made him very resentful"* (BE Heike A. 1050-1061). The Care Worker suggested that there were also possibly conflicts of loyalty, he was always negative about his father but *"that what the mother said also played a role"* (BE Heike A 1052-53).

She suspected that Christian's aggression was mostly the result of the absence of the unavailable father, especially in financial matters.

"I found that it was a pity that he had such unbelievable ...financial problems, right, because his father didn't help him with his student grant and didn't fill it out – the bit that he had to fill out. Because of that Christian didn't get any money for hundreds of years. Mmm, and I think it is simply typical behaviour that he learnt about, this 'not caring', and you are

irrelevant, true. I think that that was the reason for a lot of his anger" (BE Heike A. 1073-79).

The Care Worker in Italy confirmed this view:

"His father played absolutely no role in Christian's life at that time, he had no contact. In my view the father had not supported him in any way, financial or otherwise. His mother ... never included the father in discussions, I think that this father - mother - son relationship, divorce, separation, this whole triangle of father, mother, son played a role which should have been addressed therapeutically before he came to us, to clear his head. That hadn't happened" (BE Klaus B. 457-463).

3.5.4. Life skills

Christian didn't go to school during his time in the supported living group. He was admitted to a psychiatric hospital several times because of his asocial and destructive behaviour. In the intervals he followed his phantasies of violence and behaved in a threatening manner. He lacked optimism and consistent direction or life plans. In retrospect, the aim of the Care Worker in Germany was:

"My aim wasn't really that, er, Christian studied, erm, that was, in general, my personal wish, that he got a good qualification naturally, ... but I thought it was much more important that Christian found a place in society, where he can live and survive with himself. ... So that was unbelievably

important, erm, because I never saw that when I started with him" (BE Heike A. 896-901).

The Care Worker in Italy wanted to enable Christian to find *"a new optimism, a reason to survive in our society"* (BE Klaus B. 531-532).

The few support plans in the files mention as single aim the achievement of a high school qualification in Italy.

3.6. Resources of the young person and their family

3.6.1. Christian's resources

All of the service providers identified Christian's intelligence as an important resource. Implicit in this was the possibility that it would be possible to discuss with him on a cognitive level. The Care Worker in Germany also emphasised his persistence, love of order, his humour, bravery and openness for new experiences.

> *"He's like this, when he's interested in something he really gets involved and reads a lot .. and then he knows and talks a lot about it, anyway an enormous knowledge, n, mmm .. I always liked that, I think that it is a resource, to look over the edge of the plate, mmh ...naturally his intelligence anyway... that he can laugh at himself sometimes, I thought that that was very important and that helped him, I think also, helped us in a lot of difficult situations, that we could both laugh. .. anyway that when reflecting on things it was possible to talk about difficult*

themes with a bit of a grin, [...] and then I find that he often challenged himself, that is was brave. Like with the programme in Italy, like I know he was scared but he also was also open and curious about life and other people, even when he often spent a long time turning on himself and only thought about himself and again about himself, ...mmmh ... but I think that's got something to do with being able to give things a go at other times" (BE Heike A. 284-302).

Beyond that she emphasised Christian's honesty but this could have also been his impulsiveness

"Mm, openness and honesty, so Christian is really not someone who hides what he thinks. That is a really important part of his character that was something I really liked, he was also very forceful and you didn't necessarily like what came out of him unfiltered, that was Christian.,.. yeah I think it's good when you know who you're dealing with"(BE Heike A. 291-296)

The Care Worker in Italy remembered:

"Everything was there, Christian had everything. It was all... let's say all the ways in to his resources were plugged ... everything, really every resource was like filtered through a sieve, had not been not respected and ... they all had to be opened again. It was quickly apparent that Christian was a young person who in the end needed a challenge but doesn't want to be challenged because whatever had been offered to him didn't meet his picture of the world or of himself. And when these resources were tapped into, even a bit, they came

> *to the top. They only had to be <u>found</u>. They were all there, they were just <u>buried</u>. ... and yeah, that's why I can say that Christian was a young person – if I could use a metaphor – he was plastered with all sorts of things from top to bottom. All of the entrances were blocked, he had made a cocoon which stopped him from communicating with the outside world in a normal way ... and that was what we very, very quickly discovered; that every ability was there." (BE Klaus B. 90-104)*

In the end Christian's intelligence, his hunger for knowledge and his interest in discussing philosophical topics and questions about life and death provided an avenue to reach him on an emotional level.

3.6.2. Family resources

In the view of the Coordinator the family played almost no role (KO Mr S. 79-85) although Christian was only 15 at the start of the programme.

The Care Worker mentioned some basic support from the mother but she added:

> *"Although I think that he behaved in the way he did because he knew that if his mother got wind of his behaviour, it'd piss her off. Mmmh, the relationship between mother and son was extremely difficult and therefore... hard to gauge whether that was good or bad, that... the mother supported that." (BE Heike A. 358-362)*

Christian also had a good relationship with his grandmother and who supported him as much as she could.

> *"He always visited granny and I went with him. Yeah, granny was a granny just as you would imagine, so he was Christian and 'Christian is bad, but he is also my grandson and here you are, here's a bit of money, it's OK' "* (BE Heike A. 694-697)

The Care Worker got to know Christian at a time that his family and particularly his mother appeared helpless *"because, in the end she simply couldn't endure what was happening with her son. At the time I had the impression, that, ... really she had given up on him and had quite obviously focused on her daughters"* (BE Klaus B 115-117).

He perceived the mother as being frail who *"was dissatisfied with herself"* who couldn't be much support for her son. The Care Worker noticed in particular that there was an 'emotional coolness' between son and mother. *"Nothing happened between mother and son in the way that she had seen happening with other families if they haven't seen each other for a long time. I think that his mother was very careful, very judgemental about what was happening to her son. And, no, I didn't get the feeling of any emotional warmth from her"* (BE Klaus B 465-71)

3.7. Setting design

3.7.1. Care work in the supported living group (SLG) and the emergency accommodation

After Christian was referred to "Jugendhilfe Phöinix e. V." at the age of 15 for intensive social education it was decided that he should move into a newly founded supported living group. A Care Worker lived in the supported living group which received additional support from ambulant Care Workers. Christian's key Care Worker was Heike A., a social worker with many years' experience in the drug support unit in the emergency accommodation.

The coordinator confirmed that, based on the reports and history available, there was *"little to speak against an admission to the supported living group as Christian was described as able to participate in a limited way, in group living. Therefore this setting which had been newly developed and had a high staff ratio appeared to be appropriate for him [...]"* (KO Mr S. 30-33). However even at the first introduction doubts arose about the planned accommodation. These doubts increased after he moved in *"quite quickly it became clear that [...] the structure or the concept we used as a model for the support group was not the right one for Christian (KO Mr S 93-6). As time went on Christians outbursts increased and then he locked himself in his room with a member of staff, threatened to rape her and put a knife to her throat – so massively threatening (KO Mr S. 130-3).* However, this didn't prevent Christian being left in this support group for 1½ years.

The young man himself described the time as chaotic, the atmosphere as horrible and his feelings for the people he lived with as being particularly negative.

> "Ahm, so ... when I think about the time in the group then ... they are mixed feelings, mostly negative. Erm, I'll start with the positive. Looking back the positive things were ... yeah at the time I was really partying hard... so, alcohol, drugs ... erm, yeah, ... that was, a rebellious time, so I didn't go to school er, to annoy my Care Workers. ... refused to do other stuff, too like housekeeping and so on. Er, that was like a time ... sometimes I like to think back on it, because ... yeah so simply a storm and stress phase. The negative memories were that I basically hated living in that house, that was as I said ...I found it to be pretty much a hole. During the whole time I was there in this group I never had bedroom furniture. I remember that for a long time I slept on a mattress on the floor ... at the best time I had one cupboard in my room so that was a bit poor. And what I definitely hated was the other young people who lived there, who you could get on with sometimes when it was about having a secret drink or to gang up against the Care Workers ... but basically I would say that we had such different characters. .. that I didn't really like them and ... anyway, it was really chaotic"(Christian 212-230)

Part and parcel of this "chaos" were the regular confrontations with police and psychiatry:

> "And the police as well, because he always had the tendency to run amok, ... took him out of the house really violently, special operations team with drawn guns, so not nice and not nice for

him, either. [...] And what helped me at the time that, at last, at last .... I managed to make an arrangement with the psychiatric hospital which told him: Listen here, buddy, we'll spell it out for you: if you make threats then you are already crossing a line and Heike can have you sectioned and we will take you every time, and if things go too far, we will keep you in here for a really long time" (BE Heike A. 165-176).

This cooperation and the constant availability of the coordinator helped the Care Worker, who was newly in post and was sometimes unsure of how she should act to manage what she experienced as the *"permanent crisis" (BE Heike A. 572)* of the work with Christian. *"and as the work with Christian continued, I was relying on the system around and about to support me part of the way" (BE Heike A. 186-188).*

In retrospect there is the question as to what degree Christian understood that in this situation a stay in the child and adolescent psychiatric hospital was intended to help and to protect himself and others.

When the situation with Christian became increasingly uncontrollable, it became impossible to ignore the fact that the support group as form of care for this young person was not appropriate. He was expelled from the support group and moved to a youth protection place. He continued to receive ambulant care and support from his Care Worker. Initially his non-compliance continued and it was, as before, difficult to find an appropriate service. Christian couldn't or wouldn't remember this time on the street but he could remember the feelings of being lost and hopeless and talked about it:

> *"[...] so I can remember that I met with Heike in the city centre ... yeah, basically talked about the situation or about other stuff which I can't really remember and, erm ... yeah ... so, er ... yeah, that was, erm, basically street life and ... maybe you can understand what it's like if you've done it, when you are that far .. then you don't have any hope really or anything ... at the time, erh, I took drugs ... mmmh ... yeah I was really lost, I'd say looking back"* (Christian 271 – 278).

After Christian had been living on the streets for a few months he showed an interest in going back to school because he *"yeah somehow somewhere I want to make something out of my life"*. The Youth Welfare department offered one possibility as *"alternative to the street [...] well, this programme in Sweden"* (Christian 284-291).

The farm programme in Sweden and the way that it was organised suggested that it might fit Christian's needs. The programme took place within a small and manageable framework which contrasted to the SLG. The structure of the project was built around working with dogs, feeding, training and other care.

In the SLG, Christian had been consuming increasing amounts of alcohol and the isolation of the farm and the high cost of alcohol in Sweden were a further advantage.

The aim of the programme was to help Christian learn to deal with conflict where he didn't have a verbal advantage and enable him to experience new ways of improving his personal skills and his self-confidence (Source: Case file note – reasons for an experiential social education programme for Christian in Sweden). This would be done through intensive work with caring for and training sled dogs and learning to drive a sled.

After the project was described to him in detail Christian decided that he didn't want to go. The reasons: didn't feel like working, no access to school and the other young person in the programme seemed, according to his description, to be unlikeable. (Christian 236-63). *"and then the project in Italy was described and .. I was supposed to decide between the two ... that's what happened then"* (Christian 292-3)

3.7.2. Transfer to Italy

In suggesting Italy the professionals involved had taken account of Christians depressive tendencies *"We suggested Italy as a possible programme location simply to hold up a light for him, in the hope that lots of sun and warmth maybe again as well ... would have a certain influence and .. You'd have to say the programme in Italy went a lot better than in the support group in Germany"* (KO Mr S. 93-144).

In the end Christian decided to go to Italy. He had some "rather pleasant calls" with his future Care Worker and flew with his German Care Worker to Italy.

> *"It was the first time I flew, anyway the first impression was just relief, having a solid ground under my feet ... yeah the first impression was the heat, bloody bright, .. palm trees, that was C. ..yeah, then I met Klaus .. until then I had only spoken to him*

> on the phone [...] yeah Klaus and Heike and me drove into the mountains where the programme was based, the house mmm .. and the first few days he showed us around a lot, the landscape, how he worked, we spoke to each other, how he imagined the programme would work [...] it took a while before I felt a bit at home, I would say"(Christian 322-337).

And the Carer: *"Christian came to us with a colleague, a very proactive and friendly colleague, who had very carefully introduced him to the programme. That was the deciding point, he knew the colleague who came over with him and they had a very trusting relationship"* (BE Klaus B. 151-6).

3.7.3. 1:1 care in Italy

The programme location in Italy was in a rural and isolated area. According to the file it consisted of three rooms for young people, community room, a living room for the Care Worker and an office. In addition there was an outreach flat in a nearby town. Klaus the Care Worker was self-employed and worked closely with his therapist trained wife. At the tie he employed three Care Workers in rotating shifts 24 hrs a day. Every Young Person had a key Care Worker.

Klaus B. described his programme in the interview as *"a place which allows you to breathe deeply again"* (BE Klaus B. 52). He felt that one of the reasons for this was the isolated location:

> *"We have a house in a completely rural location, we live with 7*

inhabitants. This place is at least 120km from C. in an area that is so isolated that it counts as one of the most isolated places in Europe. .. [...] That's the offer, what we can give to young people: that we live near to nature together but then, when things work out, then slowly and thoughtfully lead them back into a city life, reintroduce them into our society"(BE Klaus B. 504-10).

In relation to Christian: *"That's why he couldn't just run riot. See, here you can't just amble across the town square and pull out a sword. This is the countryside, you've got chamois and wild boars, and then there's the occasional wolf in the area but people wielding swords? Not so much. This environment void of any distraction caused him to think a lot about himself and the way he lived his daily life." (BE Klaus B. 268-273)*

The pair of Care Workers also had

"a close network of support. We work together with a psychiatric service, with external psychotherapists and my wife provides a psychological and psychotherapeutic reference point right here. We can cover quite a range from Systemic to Gestalt therapy to talking and working therapy. We have our own supervisor. We have a person who has advised us for over 20 years. We have schools and training schools in our community. Yeah, that's is what we have here in our surroundings. These are primary elements for us here" (BE Klaus B. 504-510).

The decision to refer Christian to the programme, was made, as far as the Care Worker could remember, by the Youth Welfare Office and "Jugendhilfe Phöinix e. V": *"anyway, normally I have been used to having the final decision about which young people come to me...in this case it was all pretty clear that he was coming* (BE Klaus B. 19-21).

Decisive for the referral of Christian to the programme in Italy was:

> *"that the young man was in a very volatile living situation where a decision had to be made between trying to integrate Christian into a lifestyle in society in Germany or shifting the whole question abroad in order to prepare him for that life ... or the slightly different life in Germany" (BE Klaus B. 26-30).*

The Care Worker in Italy wished to offer Christian an appropriate programme:

> *"The information that I was able to access showed me that simply none of the participants knew what to do next, how they could get any further … with this special young man. Whether he should go to another youth support group, cared for in another group setting, one to one care or in a psychiatric ward. I gathered from the information that was made available that simply too little had been expected of him. In school and intellectually" (BE Klaus B. 34-9).*

The Care Worker had the impression that, at the time, the services were not adequate for young people like Christian and did not appreciate how important it was to provide an individual person centred programme.

In the preliminary talks and the first few days with Christian the Care Worker became convinced that: *"that the young man should have the opportunity to talk to and discuss with people who were prepared to adjust to his special intellectual level as well as the normal school and experiential social learning"* (BE Klaus B. 55-8). And that was basically his offer to Christian *"and then we had lots and lots of discussion about it, sometimes all night. That was exactly the right thing, no distractions"* (BE Klaus B. 267-8).

When asked what he remembered best about the programme with Jugendhilfe Phöinix e. V Christian said *"a lot and good in any case, ah, Italy because that ... was definitely the turning point for me in those years [...]"* (Christian 57-8).

3.7.4. Post programme ambulant support in Germany

After the return to Germany (Christian was of legal age and had decided to finish the programme in Italy) his care continued from Heike A. for a further year with steadily reducing hours. He slept mostly in emergency accommodation for young people and he didn't like it at all. He began to take drugs and drink alcohol. Later, with help from his Care Worker he was able to find a flat of his own.

The Care Worker assumed that the continuity afforded by her continued presence (Support Group, Emergency accommodation, transition to Italy, accompanying during the residential project and support after the completion of the project) played an important role in the success of the programme.

> "Because you don't have to start from scratch, but that is Christian, you know him, you don't have to try and get inside him, you can simply see, in any case you can honour the progress that he has made [...] so I think that it was a complete thing, I don't know how Christian, so I think it wasn't enough .. in a way, with question mark [laughs] .. but it was good that he had it, and ... whether you could have got much more out if the programme had gone on for a bit longer, I'm not so sure, but we will never know" (BE Heike A. 791-807).

The Care Worker in Italy held a different view. He answered the question about what he would do differently in the work with Christian:

> "In retrospect .. but the distance doesn't allow it ..I would have like to have continued to advise and support Christian on his return to Germany. I think that he had lots of highs and lows after he left ... I don't know what he is doing today, er, but I think that I could have made his path a little shorter because he didn't really experience support; he didn't really know how to ask for the kind of help ... that could have speeded up his progress. Then he did end up putting his foot in it again and again... " (BE Klaus B. 439-445).

Christian confirmed that the support promised at the end of his programme in Italy was insufficient in quantity and quality:

> *"[...] yes, at the time where ... I had my own flat, that I lived in for a few years,. .. Heike visited quite often, it was ... but really the support at the time through Heike was, ah I have to say this, pretty shit. That wasn't Heike's fault, it was just that I almost never saw her and could have used a bit of help sometimes"* (Christian 496-504)

3.8. The participation of the young person and his parents

3.8.1. Christian's participation

Christian himself didn't have much memory of the time when he moved into the supported living group *"so, I must honestly say that I can't remember anything … not really. I don't exactly know why I ended up there, if that was decided or if I wanted it. I don't know any more."* (Christian 76 – 79).

Obviously Christian knew what he didn't want anymore but had no idea how things should continue. The decisive factor in his decision to move into supported living was his wish to get off the street: *"Yeah [short laugh] as I see it today, I would have gone anywhere because this emergency accommodation really wasn't … so it wasn't particularly nice to have to live there and, erm, I think that that was one of the reasons I wanted to move into the supported living group.* (Christian 84-87)

As it became clear that the support group wasn't appropriate and

Christian was in danger of ending up on the street again, the search for alternatives began. In which Christian, from his general position of rejection, refused to participate. In the end he was offered the programme in Sweden: *"[...] He wanted to go to Norway or Sweden because gods like Tjor and Odin lived there and it was always properly dark"* (KO Mr S. 137-9). As a result a Coordinator from Jugendhilfe Phoenix e.V. who knew the programme well visited Christian who then made a clear decision not to take the offer up. He explained this from today's perspective thus:

> *"[...] if I remember right this guy N. from A. came to G. to talk to me about it and he told me more about the programme, at the time all I had had was a brochure, and I decided that I definitely didn't want to go .. one of the reasons was that you had to work hard, at the time I was a lazy pig, I still am. .. and the other was, I can remember really well that at the time just before living on the street, I had a bright moment and wanted to go back to school and I was told that that wouldn't be possible in Sweden to go to school and .. altogether .. I was also told that there was another young person who was .. erm .. I can't really remember what I was told, I only knew that that wasn't anybody I wanted to be cooped up with somewhere in Sweden in the middle of nowhere [laughs] and spend time with and ... and as I refused, I heard the call of the streets [laughing]."*(Christian 250-63).

By the time the offer came to go to Italy Christian was in a desperate situation without any apparent alternatives and this, according to the Care Worker, contributed to Christian's agreement.

> "Then I suggested Italy, the programme ... and I think, because he was living on the street and had always expected that people made him offers and he refused them, he sort of celebrated himself and he felt good about it. And then I think he finally understood: 'I'm only punishing myself'. I think it was very clear for him to see that he was treading water" (BE Heike A. 413-19).

The Care worker in Italy thinks that Christian made his decision about Italy when he was in a state of not being able to cope.

> "I think, at the time, Christian ... was very probably overwhelmed by the question and that other things were swirling around inside his head. I think that the offer was made and in the end he said yeah, Ok I'll do it" (BE Klaus B.13-16).

Christian wrote to the Youth Welfare Office in February 2001 to say that he wanted to go to the programme in Italy. In an interview the main reason he gave was that he hoped to finish high school.

> "Ahem, not the landscape because ... I find Sweden far more exciting, at the time I wanted to go to Sweden more,. erm, .. I can remember really well though that the main reason to go to Italy was that there was a possibility to finish my High School studies ... I know that ... that that was really the main reason ... erm ..Yeah at the time I couldn't decide, because ... somehow

> *the heart said Sweden and the head Italy, but then I moved to Italy, [laughing] more or less"* (Christian 298-305).

After he reached the age of 18, Christian strongly requested his return to Germany. He wanted to live in his own flat and manage his life by himself:

> *"Yeah, that was really stupid, maybe, to be fair, ... that the whole thing was my fault. At the time I had a really good relationship with Klaus and he had suggested, and I wanted, too at the beginning, that I spend a bit more time in Italy after I was 18 to finish a couple of school exams and my secondary school leaving certificate [rem: A-levels, to be able to go to university]. Erh, as the unexpected conclusion of the programme, I don't really think of it as unexpected conclusion it was the Youth Welfare Office in L. who called it an unexpected conclusion. So, in short I was going to be 18, I had the feeling that I'd spent a lot of time in care and somehow I wanted to do my own thing and then I decided without thinking about it that I wanted to go back to Germany, because I knew [clears his throat] at last I can have my own flat, as an 18 year old I had a right and then I can do my own stuff at last.. and.. yeah, that was the reason for me to end the thing in Italy"* (Christian 441-53).

The Care Worker in Italy said that he respected Christians wish to return to Germany because he felt that it was appropriate at his current stage of development. In his view it was the result of the work together in Italy. After careful observation and weighing up the different reasons he supported Christian.

> *"and ... the support that we offered him, it wasn't enough anymore because he saw, he is getting older. He needed to face challenges and he wanted to face them, namely the secondary school leaving certificate and lots and lots of other stories" (BE Klaus B. 366-69).*

The Care Worker found it difficult that Christian's decision was not met with the same understanding and support:

> *"What I would do differently ... Yes, I would support him a lot more in his life journey ... As he detached himself from us, disengaged from us, I did hear in the background that from Jugendhilfe Phöinix e. V's point of view they would have liked him to stay for longer, because he said in the Youth Welfare Offices at the last support plan meeting, before he left us, he wanted to do the secondary school leaving certificate or think about other qualifications, that he wanted to <u>do</u> them in Italy. And... after we came back to Italy from the support plan meeting, after this meeting in Germany he reflected on a lot of things and we had a lot of serious discussions and afterwards he said <u>for himself</u> that it was all good and wonderful but he had to learn to stand on his own two feet. He said he didn't want to depend on a warm and fuzzy social safety blanket that sheltered him from everything" (BE Klaus B. 417-28).*

He wished that participation was more encouraged for young people and that, in general, they were taken more seriously *"I think that .. maybe listen a little more carefully when a young person says, I understand, to take that more seriously and say OK, let's try and do it together"* (BE Klaus B. 432-434).

Today Christian is very critical of his decision:

> *"Mmm, that was the most stupid thing I have ever done in my life, that's clear, it was really stupid, because the programme was funded for longer, erm I would probably have finished my studies by now and wouldn't be stuck in the last year of an apprenticeship, more or less, erm, yeah, so ... it was stupid because ... the time after Italy was bloody horrible and .. OK but that was something I stuffed up myself"* (Christian 469-474).

3.8.2. Participation of the parents

The mother as legal custodian for Christian had signed her agreement to the decision to put him in the supported living group and for the ambulant care (cp. KO Mr S. 20-22). This and further collaboration was mainly formal. For example she agreed to the sectioning of Christian into a psychiatric hospital which the Care Worker found helpful. Despite this there were ambivalent answers to questions about the degree to which her involvement was felt to be supportive:

> *"Mmm, difficult. .. OK the mother naturally accepted [clears*

> *throat] the programme and supported it. What the family, the mother... [...] It was irrelevant for Christian what his parent said... Although I think he sometimes behaved in the way he did [...] to piss his mother off. [...] I think she just said yes to avoid ... getting more involved .. [...] .. I think that Christian's mother visited him just once when he was on the programme. That shows somehow what sort of relationship it was. And you can't call that particularly supportive" (BE Heike A. 354-73).*

Christian spoke for his mother when he said, with regard to participation:

> *"[...] besides my mother told me a few days ago that .. she has very negative memories of the time because she felt that she was completely left out of the picture by Jugendhilfe Phoenix and the Youth Department, she didn't really know what was happening or what I was doing"* (Christian 200-3).

Before the planned interview with the mother she confirmed what her son said. Unfortunately, the interview didn't take place as the mother broke off contact with the interviewer unexpectedly.

On the whole the impression remains that whilst the mother was informed about decisions which she then agreed to, she was not involved much in the process of the decision making.

3.9. The quality of the relationship between the young person and the support services

3.9.1. Christian - ambulant care worker in Germany

This relationship was very complicated and ambivalent. On one side Christian was deeply emotionally attached to the Care Worker but on the other side it was a relationship characterised by power and control. It is possible that Christian was prepared to protect the exclusivity of their relationship with every means possible including violence and continually tested Heike's resilience. He retained a pattern of behaviour that couldn't be changed. Heike's hypothesis was that Christian sought, through her, to work through his ambivalent feelings about women without completely succeeding: *"simply because he was working with his issues with his mother through me,"* (BE Heike A. 495-6)

Both Christian and Heike mentioned the contradictions in their relationship:

> *"mmm, yeah, I was asked at the time whether .. Heike was, somehow. .. the right Carer for me and um, .. I find it really difficult to answer, because, erm .. somehow at the time I didn't really respect her .. but despite everything we had 'n... intensive relationship, feelings wise. I did really trust her and I think with another Care Worker who might have been a bit stricter, that wouldn't have worked at all, so from <u>today's</u> view then I would have landed on the streets a lot sooner"* (Christian 681-8).

The relationship to Heike in the SLG:

> "[...] You could call it a love/hate relationship, because .. sometimes we got on really well .. and sometimes I really wanted her dead and I suspect that, despite all of the professional distance, that she thought the same of me" (Christian 160-4).

> The Care worker added: "[...] that was a sick relationship, but a sick relationship is still a relationship [laughs]" (BE Heike A. 332-4)

Over and above this there is evidence that there was a role change between the Care Worker and the Young Person. It wasn't the professional Care Worker supporting the anxious young person but it wass the young person, excellently trained to be empathetic by his mentally ill mother, who supported the Care Worker:

> "he was also .. empathetic, mm, for example [...] he held my hand in the airplane because I was scared and .. then I noticed that it was just as sweaty as mine so he must have been scared too [laughs]. Yeah but he has got something, he can be very empathetic when he wants to be and also respect when he sees that somebody is doing something, that somebody is overcoming their barriers" (BE Heike A. 300-13).

Christian provoked Heike with sexual behaviour who insisted in contrast that

> "for me, in retrospect it was simply because I thought, he was

always asking me, Heike, what would you do if you fell in love with me? Nay, I said, I won't fall in love with you. 'What would you do if?' And I said 'I would, if I was really infatuated, which is really, really and absolutely unlikely [laughs], then I would give up my job. And then I would marry you' and [laughs] we used to make jokes where then Mr S. always thought that Christian was in love with me ... and that's why he asked. And I used to completely reject that assumption and said never, never, he isn't in love with me. I would feel that, that's a different feeling" (BE Heike A. 853-862)

It was important for Heike that *"that you show him he's somebody you can put up with"*. She tried to do this *"in the first instance through patience and humour"*. Of the same importance was: *"that somehow I was clear that boundaries are needed and that they had to be set"*. Effective means of achieving that were through laying criminal charges or having him sectioned into a psychiatric hospital. And further: *"I think that was, that was often the question, how much can you put up with and I think I could put up with a lot and did, mm I think that that was lucky for him* (BE Heike A. 201-12).

The question arises, though, to what extent the Care Worker and Jugendhilfe Phöinix accepted that, in the process, the Care Worker's boundaries were overstepped:

"So I have this thought process, do I carry on, do I not carry on, he always managed to get me. There were always moments where I thought no, not with me. I can't do that, I'll quit,. .. Mmm ... but somehow I always pulled myself together, I think

> *partly he was lucky that he was the first young person I worked with and I thought a bit – I must be able to do it. Today I see it differently but then I was ambitious and thought it can't be, I must be able to do it and I have to be able to put up with it. ... and that's why I kept going and then there were situations, ... where you saw that he was in need and... somehow you can do it* (BE Heike A. 149-59).

The Coordinator respected the 'persistence' of the Care Worker:

> *Yes I was just speaking about the Care Worker Heike A. I think that with her he had somebody [...] and consistently, regardless of the crisis or situation he found himself in, whether it was in the psychiatric hospital, the supported living group, even after threatening her with a knife and locking her up ... the Care Worker never gave up. Instead she continued and stayed with him through all of the highs and lows. I think that was something that he had never experienced in that way. The continuity, that gave him some sort of stability. Erm, you have to give the colleague in retrospect a lot of praise and a ... yes, a lot of praise"* (KO Mr S. 150-61)

3.9.2. Christian - care worker in Italy

The male Care Worker in Italy was a father figure for Christian and, together with his wife, offered him a family atmosphere. Christian obviously very much enjoyed the exclusiveness of the relationship. The Care Worker was able to confront him, he was clear and consistent and Christian found him to be well educated and that he could learn from him. These are the characteristics which Christian often mentioned in the interview:

> "[...] Klaus had a big influence on me, basically, you could say he was almost a father figure for me ... erm, from the beginning, in the beginning or occasionally we had small disagreements ... with him but not really arguments, no big ones anyway" (Christian 347-52).
>
> "What I really liked was that it was basically a family atmosphere" (Christian 347-352)
>
> "I can remember [laughs] we used to argue a fair amount, erm ... what we used to argue about, they were basically, I would say little things, because he did, erm, somehow challenge me to make decisions or find my way and .. I hadn't really had that before I went there" (Christian 331-35).
>
> "I built up a really intense relationship with Klaus, I had one with Heike too, erm, but limited because of the situation, but Klaus B is a person who is well educated and that had an effect of me, I learnt a lot [...] and because Klaus's had the programme in several houses most of the time I lived with him in the same house and. .. because it was in a very rural setting, it was very isolated, that was in the middle, yeah it was just forest and mountains, ... it was a very intensive sort of care, yeah, basically it was almost like family life... that did me a lot of good, I would say in retrospect" (Christian 581-94).

The Care worker Heike A met Klaus B. in Italy and remembered:

"And this Care Worker there was a...was a action man not your typical educator, nah, but more like 'Yeah, come over here, I'll show you something'". And he made it clear 'not this, not that, not that, either [laughs] but that there, yes, we will do that and that' and you could tell Christian was taking a shine to it" (BE Heike A. 462-65)

"[...] In that week in Italy I saw that he was simply attracted to the other Care Worker, just because he was a man (BE Heike A. 1062-3).

According to the Care Worker – together with the good weather and countryside – talking together about the things that interested and occupied Christian was important to developing the relationship:

> *"and I introduced him to what we could offer, at the beginning I don't think he could make much of it because he had had too much experience in his life of being rejected. So couldn't immediately accept it. That developed during the first discussions, that he realised that he had ... with me, with us here in the house a basis for discussing things that was also on <u>his</u> level and <u>his</u> themes that were going around in <u>his</u> head. He had somebody to listen but in me, he also had a partner in dialogue who was prepared to reach out to him and couldn't be fooled. I say that from his point of view because I think that what he read at the time, Alexander Crowley, lots of Lovecraft, Timothy Leary, Carlos Castaneda and a few other Intellectuals , were, on the whole in general not very well known among people of the pedagogical persuasion. ... I am one of those people who has concerned himself with lots .. yes, also philosophical subjects. I'm confident in saying that he had*

found his <u>master</u>."(BE Klaus B. 67-80)

Klaus felt that Christian had found a father figure in him and had become *"fully fledged"* (independent) (BE Klaus B. 391) and emphasised, in common with Christian, the sustainability of the relationship:

> *"Christian is a young man who has now left us but has never lost contact. He ... phones and, again and again ... he stresses that it was exactly <u>this</u> stay with us that ... opened his eyes"*(BE Klaus B. 388-90).

> *"Christian came on holiday twice to Italy and introduced the Care Worker and his wife to his girlfriend as the surrogate parents he had always wished for as a young man. He has reflected in retrospect and shows himself to be thankful – invited the pair of Care Workers 5 or 6 years later to a meal - that was his conclusion and farewell"* (BE Klaus B. 391-409).

3.9.3. Christian - other professionals

Supported living group (SLG)

It is noticeable that Christian felt there was difference between the Care Worker who was working with him and the other Care Workers, especially the night staff:

> *"with the other Care Workers .. I don't know, how did I experience them? Yeah they were just there. Sometimes I had*

good conversations with them. Erm, I had a good connection to some of the night staff, the people who supervised us at night. We, that's the other young people as well, got on with them often much better than the Care Workers, that was probably because... they didn't try to discipline us [laughs]" (Christian 184-190).

Whilst Christian was in Italy he confided to Heike A. that he had had a sexual relationship with one of the night staff for 6 months. *"[laughs] Erm, yeah, erm, I think that you know that I had a sexual relationship with one of these night staff, that went on for about 6 months but then it petered out [...]"* (Christian 190-3).

The Care Worker also remembered that Christian had a special relationship with his therapist.

"somehow he managed to have a strangely good relationship with Christian .. I was always a bit confused because he had simply stopped being professional and carried on meeting him privately and I found that strange. Mmm, nevertheless he was somebody that Christian was very fond of and who he listened to a bit. Or at least could make him think about what he was doing. .. in the phases where he was just aggressive and unmanageable and couldn't be persuaded with money or through angry words.. he had a bit more luck that he was more able to reach him, and, for various reasons I brought him into my work. So I told Christian that it was important that he talked to someone and asked him if he knew where or who with. And he said directly,' this guy' [...] Mmm, the therapist

> died later, fell down whilst he was climbing, so that was really bad for Christian. He was important" (BE Heike A. 748-69).

Christian didn't mention the therapist in his interview.

In Italy

> "Mmm, there was another Care Worker... D.R. he was called. I had a very good relationship with him for a while because ... he was still very young, also a bit, erm, I don't mean it in a bad way, freaky ... I got on really well with him .. and with the other Care Workers really ... not as much but I didn't have much to do with them, because the project was spread out between a number of locations that were quite far apart ... and I didn't have much to do with them, seldom really saw them" (Christian 377-85).

Klaus B said that Christian was strongly focused on him and his wife, he didn't mention D.R:

"We were the main people involved with Christian, he did work with other colleagues but ... mainly with us. I can't really remember that he did much with the other colleagues. The main thing was that he did things with _us_" (BE Klaus B. 385-88).

3.9.4. Relationships with others

The Care Worker Heike A. reports that Christian developed a friendship with her boyfriend, U.

"[...] and father figure, he was always looking for somebody. He really looked up to 'U' my boyfriend. They met whilst we were doing something together at the weekend, Christian thought that this Irish guy was awesome ..awesome, although we have always asked ourselves what did he find so awesome? [laughs]. But maybe it was, for example, that my boyfriend is not in any way an educator. And if Christian accepted anyone saying 'Christian you've drunk one beer too many' then it was my boyfriend, not me" (BE Heike A. 496-502).

This could be evidence that, even before the Programme in Italy, Christian was looking for and needed a male person to relate to.

3.10. Process design between the young person and the support services

3.10.1. Social behaviour

The most important interventions in this area were based on a relationship made up of boundaries, persistence, sanctions, positive reinforcement, reflection, argument, transparency and dependability. The following quotations from the interviews with the Coordinator and the Care Worker illustrate this:

"It was always extremely difficult to know what was going on with him. I don't know how many times he was sectioned, with the doctor, with the police, with a Care Worker, without a Care Worker, me alone, the Care Worker alone. I really don't know

how often it happened, I think that I was with him in the psychiatric hospital alone 6 to 8 times where we had to (and wanted to) put him for short periods because he appeared to be massively dangerous to himself and others (KO Mr S 100-15).

" [... that was ... often a to-ing and fro-ing, .. it wasn't about shoving him into a psychiatric hospital but about getting some form of diagnosis. But it was all very, very difficult (KO Mr S.188-90).

"so he injured himself horribly ... he was dangerous to others ... and for me it was important that ... he developed ways of behaving ... with other people and to get on with them at least adequately. At least so that he didn't face resistance from everywhere and didn't end up just lonely" (BE Heike A. 901-5).

"and for me it was so that I said OK I'll carry on working with him but I have to find a way for me to make it clear that certain things are not acceptable and I won't allow it and I will show you a clear boundary."(BE Heike A. 168-71).

"And I think that it was very important that if I said something that I stood by it, both positive and negative, mmm, that I was somebody who in quotes 'punished' the breaking of boundaries through, for example, sectioning. But I also honoured him when he really did something good or when it was just going well, an afternoon without stress. Sometimes I bought a pizza or a doner (kebab) and said, 'OK you don't have to cook, I'll get something'"(BE Heike A. 243-9).

"[...] and what I did well was offer him a relationship and ... discuss it with him. Yes I sent you to the funny farm ... but you *can see you are here again [laughs]. So reflecting, sticking with my decision, discussing, because of course he was indignant, but I could explain why I did it and that I would do it again if needed ... and I think that after a certain point ...I am very honest and had a situation with Christian once where we standing nose to nose because I had lost my temper ... and where he had been threatening for hours, when, at some point I said 'you know, you just talk, now bring it on' ... I was so angry at that moment that I said to myself 'even if he hits me [laughs] I'm not scared'. And I think he realised that ... then he sat down and banged his head against the door and I said stop doing that [laughs]. And then for the first time he withdrew, came back later, it was a little uncomfortable, and embraced me from behind and I thought, O shit, he will strangle me now. And then he said 'Heike, I'm sorry'. He had never done that before. It was really as if this extreme confrontation and knowing that I wasn't scared ... that helped I think to stay firm"* (BE Heike A. 216-236).

In relationship to the diagnosis of narcissistic and depressive elements in Christian, the Care Worker in Italy said:

"and when you they are there, you have to develop ways of behaving and living with the young person that enable them to get out of this way of perceiving the world. Even a narcissistic approach to the world can be changed ... this narcissistic view of yourself can lead to very, very severe personality disorders if they are recognised but not treated" (BE Klaus B. 139-143).

In Italy the Care Worker's strategy was to meet Christian on his own terms and discuss 'the blackest subjects in the world' to motivate him to participate in the programme that could be *"one of the few last chances that Christian had to avoid sectioning into a psychiatric hospital"* (BE Klaus B. 180-5).

Christian was asked to reflect on the impression that he gave other people – this was assisted by the warm spring weather, wonderful landscapes and friendly people that had its own obvious set of rules.

> *"and he had to realise that it is really tiring to walk around with a stony face when the people around him are smiling all the time. He came to the realisation that it is really tiring, when he is the only one not wearing light clothes. He suffered and decided that he couldn't stick with it. That triggered a crisis"* (BE Klaus B. 203 – 34).

Particularly at dusk Christian sought out the Care Worker to talk. He valued his knowledge.

> *"He hadn't had that before and that was the offer I made him. Exactly the thing that is atypical for a programme like this. To have this new experiences with me. And above that I found Christian's level of dialogue ... which he obviously enjoyed"* (BE Klaus B.237-41).

They moved on from Christian's death phantasies to talk about Goethe, Schiller, Shakespeare and philosophical subjects. The Care Worker had *"to work hard to remember these sorts of literature"* (BE

Klaus B. 259-60).

Christian was fascinated, the Care Worker thinks today, that he prepared for these discussions *"and over and above that began to be annoyed that he <u>couldn't maintain his stony face</u>"* (BE Klaus B.244-5).

3.10.2. Emotional maturity

Christian was able to experience normality in his relationship with his Care Worker Heike and her partner despite all of the problems with threats and overstepping boundaries. He was supported and accompanied through his regressive phases. It is likely that, as a result of the relationship(s) he gained on emotional maturity and appropriate bonding experiences. *"I took him with me, I went with him to a Nightwish concert because he really wanted to go with me to a concert"* (BE Heike A. 706-11).

> *"that simply made him happy, to do such a normal thing and taking part in something, I think that he simply experienced being respected by U., that he belonged a bit. From then on, I used to do that a lot more, if he behaved, that he could come along. I think that was important, that he could spend time with me together, those things make for good memories, when you have been with somebody to a concert and sung this song together. In bad moments that helps when you can look back and think, ahh, she not only Heike who has me sectioned but also Heike who I go to a concert with and who sings with me yes, [...] I think that he often reined himself back because it was*

me "(BE Heike A. 716-728).

" and of course our discussions, they weren't always threatening, I had a lot of moments when I had really exciting & interesting conversations with him. They were a lot of fun. Often we had situations where we had to roll around laughing. And I think that was something I could always look back on and say, yeah I have that too and he's not just always the one running after me wielding a sabre [laughs]"(BE Heike A. 188-94).

Christian was very anxious and unsure about the transition to Italy:

"it was a bit difficult, I stayed there for a week .. because of Christian, because it was clear that he was scared and because we didn't want to jeopardise the whole thing, mmm [...] and then every evening I brought Christian to bed, every evening he was scared, that was really obvious where I thought he is showing his feelings .'You are not allowed to go away, you have to stay here, stay with me here, don't leave me alone .. I don't want to, I'm afraid. And then you won't want to know me anymore, you will be happy to get rid of this swine'. 'I said ‚yes, Christian, part of me is relieved but also because for our relationship we need a bit of a break [...] And I think you need this here, too so you can develop', but 'no you must stay' [laughs]. So we thought' O dear O dear, the day that I leave that could get bitter. But somehow we managed to arrange it in a pleasant and humorous way, we celebrated our parting but then I made a lot of small games like Man or Mouse. Simply, it was good that he could show it so openly but then really extreme again that he went into regression again. And then you had to say 'you are the man' [...] simply so that bit *wasn't so dramatic, and then it was OK and I told him that we could write and that I would be providing the after care and I look forward to it and we won't lose contact"* (BE Heike A. 465-91).

Emotional development was also planned for Italy and the impression is that the isolation and peace of the location and living with a male Care Worker made this a possibility.

"he was able to make up for lost time, he could chop wood and sweat, he was allowed to make wooden swords, spears, use bows and arrows. All of the things that he should have done ten years before in his childhood before coming to us at 16. He never had any of those experiences so that they had always become an issue again. .. You have to imagine there is a young man sitting in front of you who wants to talk about Lord of the Rings because he is just reading the book and at the same time runs around outside with a sword, with a wooden sword that he carved himself. .. often the two pictures don't fit together and, because he was intelligent, because he was a really <u>intelligent</u> person, he was able to replay his childhood very quickly, in particular what a difference it makes to develop hand eye coordination. He was able to develop more or less through play, making things, in running around, pottering about. In general so that he could discover his interest in handicraft.(BE Klaus B. 317-29).

Family relationships

The memories of his relationship with his mother during his stay in the supported living group and the short time on the street in Germany is, for Christian:

> "not very much, because at the time when I was living on the street, erm ... it was winter and very cold ... and ... my mother didn't really let me in to her flat, or at least not often, apart from one situation, where I, as a result of the cold and having nowhere to live, got pneumonia. I was allowed to recover in her flat which was really pleasant [short laugh] and apart from that nothing especially. Looking back I would say that she didn't want any contact with me" (Christian 309-16).

Even though in hindsight Christian describes the contact to his mother as being negative, it is worth noting that at a time of weakness (pneumonia) his mother offered to help him and he was able to accept that help.

It may be the case that during the programme in Germany it was actually helpful that he didn't have much contact with his mother. In Italy, with the support of a valued and male person he was able to experience everyday conflict resolution and behaviour which supported the development of bonds with other people. This made it possible for him to use these new skills in his relationship with his mother so that:

> "the relationship that consisted naturally of telephone calls and occasional letters, had improved tremendously, perhaps with the guidance of Klaus ... erm ... who made it clear to me

> *that at some point I had to return to Germany ... and that it would be nice maybe, somehow, to get on better with my mother .. ermm .. yeah the relationship with my mother, as I said, improved. When we had to go to a meeting in Germany to discuss the support plan, ... I remember, that must have been January, I spent a few nights at my mother's ... and ... remember the time as being pleasant although I can't really say exactly what we talked about or not, ... hmm but they are positive memories"* (Christian 389-400).

The absence of quarrels in the relationship with his mother was obviously a new and valuable experience for Christian. It is not known whether Christian also worked on his relationship to his father or stepfather.

3.10.3. Life skills

Christian had not been to school during his stay in the supported living group and whilst living on the street and the aim of completing his education was an important aspect of his decision to go to Italy. The Care Worker in Italy took this very seriously and provided the required support.

> *"What was new for me was that ... mmm, he had expectations, [..] he expected that somebody on his programme had to do something. I know that at the time, despite what I said I didn't really take school seriously at the beginning but ... Klaus always*

> insisted that I didn't come to a standstill. So the minimum was to work in the fields with a neighbour of his who is a farmer or to do something in the house or garden or, the alternative, school" (Christian 352-59) "I generally did my schoolwork with Klaus, .. apart from a short time when an intern did the school stuff with me"(Christian 375-77).

Christian described learning with Klaus as positive in retrospect. Together with the evening discussions about literature and philosophy, this was a suitable way of working with him. Christian had problems though with physical work. Whilst taking part in a work experience at a vineyard the following happened:

> "[...] he managed it for one and a half days and then this young man fell apart in front of me and said that he couldn't manage it any more. Eight hours in one go harvesting grapes, 'I can't do it, I'm not made for it', he said. That was the first time he experienced that although he was strong and sporty, he wasn't able to manage an 8 hour working day. [...] Yes, that showed him that he had to use his head if it didn't work straight away with his hands. He had to learn what skills the mind provided and how that knowledge could be transferred to the workplace" (BE Klaus B. 331-44).

Alluding to Nadolny's 'The discovery of slowness', the Care Worker describes Christian's psychomotor skills development process:

"Christian could see the ball flying through the air but he couldn't <u>catch it.</u> It was the same in other areas, intellectually he knew exactly how to do something but he <u>couldn't</u> transfer it into physical action. No, he was <u>strong</u>, and sporty, he had practised martial arts before and afterwards, he started to do lots of things. It was the first time, for example through archery that he managed to improve his hand-eye coordination... to see the arrow flying through the air. He learnt to use his hands effectively through this and similar activities. (BE Klaus B. 598-605).

3.11. Stakeholder collaboration

The Care Worker Heike A. described the partnership working with the Coordinator as close. The work was in 'permanent crisis' and she needed and looked for support and *"was <u>always</u> able to talk to someone"*. She was new in the post and was bit unsure how she should cope with Christian. On the whole she experienced working together with the Coordinator as supportive *"there was always an opportunity for a sharing and exchange of views which was .. good [...] satisfactory"* (BE Heike A. 555-92).

Klaus B. was not so satisfied and felt that the specific way they worked in the programme was not recognised. The colleagues at "Jugendhilfe Phoenix e.V." had listened to him and he was able to bring in suggestions, but "the organisation hadn't understood at the time what questions they should ask". *"He didn't have the feeling that, .. yes that, they had tried to understand the specific features of the individual programmes, or grappled with understanding our programme in Italy"* (BE Klaus B. 545-58).

3.12. Conclusion of the programme and ongoing support

Christian, in his interview, reported that, at a Case Conference just before his 18th birthday, Klaus had suggested that he should stay in Italy for a little longer to finish his secondary school qualification and possibly to do his general qualification for university entrance. But as Christian reached his 18th year he had the feeling that he wanted to be independent at last and live alone and *'wanted from one second to another to return to Germany [...] I believed that now the world was my oyster* (Christian 464).

The Youth Department defined this as an unplanned end to the programme and as a result the Care Worker reacted angrily, were appalled and disbelieving, They weren't impressed by this *"to-and-fro game"* (Christian 464). When asked what he would have needed on his return to Germany he answered *"(Christian 464).* When asked what he would have needed on his return to Germany, Christian said:

> *"Hmm, yeah, a bit more time with Heike would have been good, more talks, because... basically, it was good, I've put myself in this situation but it was like jumping in the deep end, because I didn't really manage by myself. I was cared for for years and then suddenly it was all gone and ... I don't know,*

> *there was somehow no helping hand there for me and that is what I was used to over the years" (Christian 509-515).*

The Care Worker believed that the conclusion of the programme made sense in terms of motivating him to act independently.

> *"I Think that Christian could have used further support .. but I have a bit of a fear that that he sort of went back to his old game. ... and in the end it was good for Christian, having to depend on himself a bit more and to have to tell himself, so I am going to do that and that. Otherwise he just would have sat there and let himself be served, too. So, that I had to check everything he did. Mmm, to understand that he isn't little Christian any more but now an adult" (BE Heike A. 513-19).*

In reading this one could definitely come to the conclusion – as hinted at in Chapter 3.7.4 – that the staffing of the after care through ambulant Care Workers from the supported living group and the emergency accomodation may not have been the best solution in the circumstances because they represented the time from before the stay in Italy. Christian had the tendency, as a result of his highly complicated and ambivalent care relationship (see Chapter 3.9.1) to return to be 'little Christian'. The conclusion could be drawn that working with a new, male Care Worker would have prevented his return to his old patterns of behaviour or would have provided an opportunity to reflect. In this context, Heike A. pointed out that Christian had another need, that he shared with other young people: to be able to get support in post programme emergencies.

> "I find it a shame that there isn't anything like that where you can say, OK if it gets really bad ... in real crises, we will put in a few more hours. He had a phase when he was really ill with schizophrenia, after the end of the programme when I thought that ... actually we should ... provide a few more hours of support. I did it by telephone and did more than I would normally do, hours of talking in the evenings ... but because he really needed it and I thought OK I can't bring it over my heart to say, listen, I don't get paid for this anymore, talk to your mother" (BE Heike A. 513-29).

3.13. The impact of the support and its effects as seen by the interviewees

When asked what had changed as a result of the work with "Jugendhilfe Phöinix e. V", he only speaks of the programme in Italy. He often mentioned the healing power of the landscape, the living situation in Italy and a close relationship with the male Care Worker:

> "Erm, yes, Italy was a completely new beginning for me ... the difference, as I've said already, was the family atmosphere. The time before Italy was exactly the opposite. One had somehow, I felt very ... lonely, also maybe somehow ... I know, yes I don't think the phrase is quite right but abandoned although that probably wasn't the case. That was the difference anyway. I

> liked being in Italy, like I said it was a magnificent landscape, it was a beautiful house. I built a very intensive... relationship with Klaus, I had that with Heike, too. However, Klaus is someone who is ...very well educated and that rubbed off on me, I learnt a lot" (Christian 574 84).
>
> "Mmm, it might sound a bit esoteric but I often dream of it because it was a lovely landscape and I often dream of making a pilgrimage through the landscape somehow ... I dream of that often" (Christian 619-22).
>
> "basically ... I would say that Italy rescued me and that was simply because of the support from Klaus, who was my personal Care Worker" (Christian 344-47).

Klaus B. emphasised the changes in his mentality, *"The sun rose in his head"* (BE Klaus B. 371).

3.13.1. Social behaviour

The Care Worker in Italy aimed to deconstruct Christian's world view and to develop a new life plan with him and this obviously worked. Two quotes illustrate this:

> "It may sound a little pompous but somehow ... the belief in the future, because, before my attitude was that there was no future, I had that again later, as mentioned I fell down a very deep hole but ... yes, what influenced me ... I came out of Italy

with a different outlook on life ... I learnt a lot, I experienced a lot in Italy, erm ... and it was simply, I forgot to mention, afterwards I visited Klaus quite a few times, amongst other visits once with my girlfriend at the time, the lady from L. and [...] it was simply, it was very strengthening to simply <u>think</u> of Italy, because it ... somehow was a good time despite all the highs and lows .. I learnt a lot, seen a lot and got around a bit ... and erm, it simply, partly gave me a feeling of inner strength or peace ... looking back on it" (Christian 503-14).

"in the end we managed to churn up Christian's view of the world and of life completely, and he realised, I'd like to say, like igniting him, I think we lit the right fuse to give him the optimism to take his life in his own hands, to laugh, to live, to not see everything in black and white, also to see the greys, to carry on, to believe in himself, also to believe in his own strength, not to give up. I think that that is what he learnt with us and for him ... we have talked afterwards ... and he said it was exactly that. He said 'With you the fuse was lit for another different life'. Which isn't unusual – that's the point of a programme, or can be, to find a new optimism, a will to survival in our society" (BE Klaus B. 522-32).

To this day, Christian has maintained regular contact to Heike A. and she is happy to see that *"OK, somehow he is getting on well, and is doing his thing and isn't delinquent any more. He doesn't have a thousand charges filed against him ... looking back, that is very satisfactory"* (BE Heike A. 917-19). She still sees his *"bad moments"* and thinks that *"there are things which he might think about again later in life, to have therapy ... or grapple with in another way but, he is managing" (BE Heike A. 944-48)*.She adds:

"[...] I think, when he looks inside himself then .. I think he is convinced that he learnt something, maybe he would say that he has learnt to get on with people, to follow his goals better, maybe to see life as such in a more positive light" (BE Heike A. 944-48).

3.13.2. Emotional maturity

The Care Worker believed that Christian:

"has found a place which he likes to remember, that he found people who he likes to remember, who he still likes to ring and meet [...] and I believe that he still sees Phöinix as a place he can still find a harbour. He knows that if he rings me and says ... it's all falling apart, then I would never say, I don't care and the same goes for the Care Worker from Italy, he wouldn't say 'tell your hairdresser', no. Mmm, and as a result that he knows that he has found a sort of second home. Something that gives him a bit of security. So the rescue net is still there, it's not so taut but that now it wouldn't be a complete free fall. So if he has a problem with his family or something like that then there are still people who are sympathetic and I believe he knows that" (BE Heike A. 944-69).

3.13.3. Family relationships

With the help of his Care Worker, Christian was able to consolidate his relationship with his mother during the programme and in particular during his stay in Italy. *"I think that he was strongly rejected before he came to us. During his time with us that was put into more perspective. ... I have to say that he is far more open to discussion about particular things, his family too and his environment"* (BE Klaus B. 119-21).

Christian organised the contact between the interviewer and his mother which suggests that there is still a bond between them but little is known about the quality of that contact. At the time of the interview there was still no contact with his father. Christian hasn't even received the completed forms from his father that he needs to apply for a student grant. (cp. BE Heike A. 1074-76)

3.13.4. Life skills

Christian achieved his secondary school diploma (rem: comparable with finishing high school/ comprehensive school in the UK) whilst in Italy (cp. Christian 362-363), learnt some important everyday skills like washing, cooking and so on. (cp. BE Klaus B. 429-30) and has worked out a career plan:

> *" Mmm .. yeah, the first thing I want to say is that there are a few things I learnt that help me today, practical things. Klaus had his own workshop, and ... I learnt through Klaus, he put lots of value on teaching young people to develop some handyman skills. That goes from repairing things in the house*

> to building things or even basic craft skills, yes, how do I saw properly or file properly. In retrospect that has helped me when I am working, that was always in the trades. I'm training now as a craftsman and I must say the interest in doing that was stimulated by Klaus, or at least the ability to do them" (Christian 630 – 40).

At the end of the programme the Care Worker Heike A. had the feeling that Christian was on a good path. He had learn not to throw in the towel, not to give up, to stay on the ball and he understood that he can use his intelligence. He has friends and, at times, a lot of fun:

> "Mmm, that's why I had the feeling [...] that he is on the right path [...] and ... that was enough for me. Naturally he isn't 100%. He needs a bit longer but with what he is doing at the moment, that he is repeating that ... and he isn't throwing in the towel, I think that these are things that he's learnt, ... learnt during the programme, I won't throw in the towel, I'll stay on the ball and I won't give up so quickly, I believe a bit in myself. I think that was what we could give him. ... and [...] Maybe it paved the way for this late epiphany' I have a brain, I will make use of it, I'll do something with it'. That's what he is doing now [...] I see him in my imagination with his friends partying and having fun" (BE Heike A. 905-16).

At the end of the programme, after a failed attempt to achieve a higher secondary school diploma[15] at an adult education centre, Christian joined a work project for young adults.

> "That was a carpenter, I worked there for a year, but that finished and was difficult only because, through the time in the Adult Education Centre I had a lot of contact with drugs .. and ... yeah... through consuming so many drugs [with a little laugh] I went through an episode of schizophrenic psychosis and then I was in a psychiatry for a few months. That threw me totally and yeah [with a little laugh] that wasn't so good [...] And then ... things just carried on, I was mostly unemployed, and then decided four or five years ago to give the Adult Education Centre another try and get my certificate. ... I did that in evening classes and worked part time as a labourer in landscape gardening, evenings in the school and I finished the school and got a really good higher secondary school diploma. During the time in L., I met my now ex-girlfriend who came from L. and one thing led to another and now here I am in L." (Christian 547-565).

Christian is now repeating his third year as a trainee jewellery maker – he hadn't gone to his exam because he had missed too much time. Christian's current life doesn't sound positive *"I said to my mother a few days ago, basically I am where I was ten years ago, I only have a few more certificates in my pocket, secondary school diploma, apprenticeship finished soon, those sort of things"* (Christian 661-64).

---

[15] : Realschulabschluss, see http://en.wikipedia.org/wiki/Realschule

3.14. Christian's ideas for his future

Christian's most important plan for the next year is to finish his apprenticeship. Apart from that he dreams of completing his general qualification for university entrance and to study sometime. *"I don't know whether I can because of financial problems and I'm not 18 anymore but a bit older* (Christian 651-653).

His long term girlfriend has just left him and *"because we aren't together any more I don't really have any plans for the future"* (Christian 651-53).

3.15. Summary

Biographical details

In Christian's case the incomplete files show that the programme began without any detailed biographical information about the young man or his family. The evidence of the degree to which Christian suffered a psychiatric illness is more speculative than factual. It can be assumed that this caused the assessment of need to be more difficult.

Programme Location and design of relationships

When read side by side, the reports and descriptions from the 1½ years in the supported living group (including the time in the emergency accommodation) compared to the reports from the programme in Italy give the reader the impression that the latter provided a better fit to meet Christian's needs.

One has to ask what reasons the participants may have had for leaving Christian and his ambulant Care Worker in the supported living group and a complicated and ambivalent Care Worker relationship for so long. One idea is that the commitment of the Care Worker made up, to some degree, for the inappropriateness of the setting even though it was above her pay grade or above what she should have been expected to deal with. On the other hand one could argue that perhaps if this unfortunate setting and its implications had not existed, and especially the time on the street, the positive developments in Italian may not have happened.

However, there is evidence from the biography that this programme, consisting of an isolated rural location in a beautiful landscape and supported by a specially trained male Care Worker who could provide appropriate relationships and dialogues was a well-fitting offer. It was in this environment that Christian could, to some extent, do without his learnt behaviour strategies which had fitted the environment in Germany. He could also move away from his threatening style and gain a new optimism, view of himself, his fellow man and life in general. The descriptions provided by Christian and his Care Workers on the subject of success factors in Italy are very moving.

Lack of supervisory and technical support for the female Care Worker

Judging from the interviews it appears that the female Care Worker had to endure much more in what was an ambivalent care relationship than should normally be expected. She had to deal with Christian's childish needs and threats without any significant support. Her commitment was and should be recognised. However, it should also be noted that other than the Coordinator from Phöinix e. V. who was always accessible, to emotional or professional support through supervision was provided to the care worker and her colleagues in intensive 1:1 social education during what was a very extreme period of time. In addition, she and the colleagues in the supported living group were quite inexperienced. It was her first time providing this form of care. The fact that there was a sexual relationship between one of the night staff and Christian which went unnoticed until disclosed by the youth himself, indicates the lack of adequate supervision.

Participation – the balancing act between the welfare and the will of the young person and the resulting conflict

Christian seems to have agreed to the move into the supported living group and the transition from emergency accommodation to a programme based outside Germany because he was overwhelmed and felt that he had no alternative or point of reference. On the other hand, with the help of Phöinix, he consciously decided not to go to Sweden because he wanted to continue his education which was possible in Italy. not to go to Sweden because he wanted to continue his education. The decision to move back to Germany from Italy after he was 18 was his own and was also made consciously and independently.

The ambivalence of the Youth Welfare Office and "Jugendhilfe Phöinix e. V." about this decision indicates that the participation of the young people and their parents often leads to a contradiction between the young person's own will and their welfare. This highlights the conflict between the young person and the adults.

The question as to whether Christian's decision was appropriate and sensible remains unanswered. The further development of the young man which included failure at school, addiction and sectioning into a psychiatric hospital suggests that the Youth Welfare Office and "Jugendhilfe Phöinix e. V." were right to be concerned. It is also possible that Christian was unable to express his need for more help at the end of the programme – today he is very critical of the quantity and intensity of the support provided after the conclusion of the programme. .

4. Case Study Lena

Sources:

- File analysis
- Interviews with:
  - Lena
  - Care Worker in Portugal (BE Anna F.)
  - Coordinator (KO Ms S.)
  - Care Worker in Portugal (Fernando F.)
  - Care Worker in Germany (Ulrike L.)

4.1. Current situation

Lena was nearly 28 years old at the time of the interview and regularly and permanently employed as kindergarten teacher in a Kindergarten.

She had also taken up studying in the hope to eventually be able to move away from working with small children. *"only I haven't really decided what I want to do but hope that I can find what sort of work I want to do during my studies, what is right for me and where I belong, what interests me" (Lena 946-48)*.

Lena lived in the same flat that she moved into at the end of her programme in L. with a dog that she brought back from her stay in Portugal. She described problems with her work and with people in both a professional and personal context.

As a result of long term and traumatic sexual abuse within her own family, Lena had developed survival strategies that lead to problems in her daily work life. For example, she found it impossible to change nappies, wash out bottles or to cuddle small children. In addition, she often came to work late because she was tired. She had problems sleeping because she had difficulty sleeping in a closed room which is why she preferred to spend her nights outside. *"That is difficult, too and with the flat ... that I can't do that either, that I can't stay in the flat for long"* (Lena 853-55).

She found it difficult or impossible to develop relationships with other people and avoided personal relationships. Her colleagues and employers found this behaviour very irritating and in the past it led to her being sacked or to an early conclusion of her work contract.

Lena saw that she still had a need for therapy and was planning to start therapy soon in the hope that it would make her life easier. *"So I can manage to be like a normal person and not attract attention, so I can sleep in my flat like a normal person" (Lena 957-59).*

4.2. Case history

Source;   case files and interviews
Start of the programme   14.09.2001
Age at the beginning of the programme   18 years and ten months
End of the programme   31.12.2005
Length of the programme   4 years and 3.5 months

Care notes
14.09.2001 – 31.08.2003

Individual social education and care in Portugal. It was a full time care programme by a couple trained in pedagogy without children of their own. The location of the programme was in a family house in a rural area by the sea and near a small Portuguese village. Lena was the only young person staying there. The main method for the programme were sports activities and helping in a riding stable that provided therapeutic riding.

01.09.2003 – 31.12.2005
Ambulant care in her own flat with stepwise reduction in support (25 hours per week at the beginning reduced to 10 hours per week by the end of the project). The focus of the support was the Lena's reintegration into school and day-to-day work life and the search for an appropriate therapy as well as support in becoming more independent a variety of everyday practical activities.

4.3. History

Lena described herself just before the beginning of the programme in Portugal as *"I was like a, like hunted, I felt like a hunted animal" (Lena 117-118)*. Lena grew up in a suburb of N. in an apparently normal family (The father was an engineer with a permanent job, her mother was a housewife and there was a young brother as well). From the age of 13, Lena attracted some attention in school. At times, she came to school three hours early, she wore summer clothes in winter and winter clothes in summer and was very tired. As a result the teacher got the Youth Welfare Office and a psychologist involved to find out what was going on. It wasn't possible to find out from Lena or her parents why she was behaving so strangely *"but I never said anything because I couldn't"* (Lena 1055-56). There was a family secret that mustn't be known under any circumstances.

At the age of 16 the pressure obviously increased as Lena ran away from home *"I couldn't stand it anymore at home because it was so bad .. and then I just ran out of the door .. in the middle of the night as fast as I could because I was so scared that my father would chase after me"* (Lena 1091-95).

Lena was taken into child protection on suspicion of early and serious sexual abuse by the father and possibly other people. Lena was under immense pressure to keep it a secret. *"My father kept ringing the shelter ... and wanted to speak to me and then was always telling me what would happen if I told anybody"* (Lena 1140-43).

Lena changed several times between the shelter and home. The abuse during weekends and by the father who lay in wait for her on her way to school continued. Lena continued to be silent.

> *"I had a lot of contact again with my father, because I didn't know at all, I don't know, because I was so stupid, because that was somehow so difficult, that I had to go all over the place, I moved out of everywhere and I wasn't important anywhere and the only thing that I knew was my father"* (Lena 1210-13).

Lena lived in a child protection shelter before being referred for a programme abroad and was closely supported therapeutically by a psychologist but with only modest success with regard to getting through to her. At the same time the parents were regularly invited to case conferences but, according to the psychologist, retained their fiction of a normal bourgeois life.

When Lena showed signs of physical abuse after her weekend home visits, massive psychosomatic disturbance (vomiting, eating disorders, instances of self-harm) and barely survived a suicide attempt, the support services decided Lena should be removed from the family atmosphere altogether to protect her from further abuse. The goal was to allow her to find an internal and external rest period. This should be achieved through intensive care far away from the family environment. It was hoped that she would be able to develop trust for other people and that her psychosomatic symptoms could be reduced as well as developing new perspectives for her life.

4.4. Initiating Contact / Initiation of support

The Youth Welfare Office referred Lena to "Jugendhilfe Phöinix e. V." as a specialist in foreign programmes. The reason given for referral to a programme abroad was to prevent further abuse by the father.

The Care Worker pair F. and the Coordinator viewed Lena's files and afterwards a meeting was initiated in a Cafe to introduce Lena to Care Worker Anna F. *"One of the first questions that she asked me was 'will you really pick me up from the airport?'"* (BE Anna F. 66-7).

Lena's fear, lack of trust, vulnerability and loneliness became apparent at this first meeting. Lena was like a *"delicate duckling ... so delicately packaged, somehow completely vulnerable, completely vulnerable"* (BE Anna F. 66-7).

A Carer of the child protection shelter where Lena had lived before she went to Portugal, accompanied her on the flight and handed her over to the Care Workers at the airport. Lena only knew the Care

Workers through the short contact in the cafe. The other Carer departed straight away. There was no sensitive transition.

The abrupt transition clearly made Lena more anxious *"and it was difficult because I had to sit in the car with, with Anna and Fernando, because I didn't know what was coming next or where I was going" (Lena 91-2)*. The strange place and the foreign language were a real challenge for Lena *"that was very intimidating, together with everything else, that you don't know where you are going" (Lena 101-2)*.

Lena still found the decision to go to Portugal easy because she got a good impression of the care workers at their first meeting *"I met them and found that they were nice straight away" (Lena 177-8)*. Lena had to reassure herself hundreds of times that she was going to be picked up at the airport *"that I asked Anna hundreds of times if they were really going to pick me up in Portugal because I didn't believe it ... and she told me hundreds of times yes, yes, really, and I didn't believe it until we got there" (Lena 186-89)*.

4.5. Key themes and goals of the support

4.5.1. Problematic social behaviour

As a result of her long term abuse as a very young child by her father, Lena had very low levels of trust to other people. From her body language and her language Lena appeared to be very anxious and shy. She withdrew from all social life and was not able to allow close relationships to friends or acquaintances.

Her relation relationships with men was characterised by fear and panic and at the beginning of the programme she was unable even to share a car alone with the male Care Worker *"in the beginning she couldn't sit alone with Fernando in the car because she was scared that something would happen" (BE Anna F. 349-50).*

4.5.2. Family relationships

As a result of the continuing abuse, an immediate separation from the family was required to protect Lena and stop the abuse. The Care Worker spoke about the urgent need *"It was high time, it was high time she got out of there, definitely " (BE Anna F. 80-81).* *"The first information provided by the Youth Welfare Office was that she needed to go far away for protection. It was crucial that she be protected from her family and must therefore go far away" (KO Ms S. 21-23).*

The subject concerned the care workers both in Portugal and throughout the whole phase of ambulant care in Germany because the Father got hold of her again and again (either in reality or through re-enactments by Lena) *"and it was difficult for me, because through that I .. that my father kept writing me letters so the contact was still there"* (Lena 625-7).

4.5.3. Emotional maturity

All of Lena's life skills, that a child would normally learn by the time they are 5 years old (e.g. eating with a knife and fork, tying shoelaces etc.) were buried as a result of the permanent traumatisation *"because I was always embarrassed that I was so old and I couldn't tie my shoelaces and couldn't hold a knife and fork like normal people, I always had to hide it" (Lena 280-82).*

The description by the care workers agreed with Lena's self-assessment. The Coordinator experienced her *"almost like a wolf child who hadn't grown up with human beings" (KO Ms S. 117)* and the Anna's assessment described her as *"having stopped developing at the age of an infant" (BE Anna F. 161).* At the beginning of the programme she often regressed to an infant. *"Lena was kept sitting in the sandpit and played with toys for at least two hours" (BE Anna F. 239-40).*

4.5.4. Life skills

Lena was very motivated to study and she was very focused and thorough. This was therefore a side issue that didn't need a lot of attention during the programme because she was independently motivated.

The biggest challenge was developing and maintaining social contacts and the care workers had to insist that Lena did anything in her recreation which might lead to social interaction. The care workers continually had to deal with the lack of motivation on Lena's part to get involved in social contact. At the beginning of the programme there was no support plan, just a statement that she should be as far enough away from her family. After six months on the 6th May 2002 the following goals were agreed and minuted in a support plan:

- Removal of her total dependence on her father (sexuality, manipulation and authority)
- Catch up on life experience in a family setting – protection from her father
- New experiences in her relationships with adults and male contacts
- Reduction of anxiety, massive emotional upsets, depressions and thoughts of suicide
- Changing childish emotional behaviour to be more appropriate

for her age and level of independence
- Reduction of her strong physical reactions (vomiting, eating disorders, sleep disorders, anxiety)
- Development of positive behaviour in contact with others (amongst other things contact to animals)
- A further six months of residential support (until she was sufficiently independent, afterwards ambulant care in a single flat far away from her parents, train as a nursery nurse, planning for examinations for university entrance)

The degree of success was to be measured in terms of her independence from her father.

4.6. Resources of the young person and her family

4.6.1. Lena's resources

Lena learnt quickly and was very interested in learning and getting on.

"I noticed only, that it, that I .. want to learn a lot and that I am very inquisitive, like with Fernando, I was always absorbing his Portuguese stuff, that I wanted know a lot and that lots of things interest me, and that learning is a lot of fun" (Lena 949-52).

Lena was very intelligent, the Coordinator observed that in terms of *"cognition, she had an unbelievable, unbelievable thirst for knowledge and an unbelievable skill to summarise things, to reflect and to discuss, or to absorb things that she wasn't clear about" (KO Ms S 121-24).*

Lena's biggest resource was her will to change. In this she was very ambitious and was able to pick things up quickly:

> *"It doesn't matter what you say, you always have the feeling that she gives you 100% attention, everything you say is 100% absorbed ... she wants to learn and have a better future than she has had" (BE Anna F. 144-47).*

Lena was very strong and persistent. *"I found that this strength was a good resource because I thought if she didn't have that, this aloofness, this strength, then .. yes then maybe she wouldn't be able to survive* (KO Ms S. 110-12). Despite the very unfavourable living circumstances, that she had suffered since early childhood, she was able to find goals and develop life prospects. She had developed survival skills which protected her and enabled her to master most everyday situations.

4.6.2. Family resources

There were none, at least none that could be seen, *"I never managed to make contact with this family I was completely ignored" (KO Ms S. 137-38).* And further: *"I can't see any resources, which could have helped Lena in any way"* (KO Ms S. 155-6). Apart from Lena herself, nobody from the support services had contact with the family.

4.7. Setting design

4.7.1. First location

The residential care in Portugal was in a small family house with a garden and within walking distance of the sea. Both of the care workers were professionally trained in education. Anna F. was a nursery teacher and Fernando was a sports teacher. The programme was designed for one young person.

Fernando F. was Portuguese and grew up near where they now live. Therefore there was a strong family and community social network. Fernando offered sport and physical activities as well as vocational work which, because of the state of the house, was always required. There was a nearby riding stable which offered ride therapy was also available work related activities.

From Lena's point of view, this setting completely different to her home. It was explicitly written into the programme that the important thing was that she received a lot of attention and that there was always somebody there for her. *"That we would always be there for her was the best thing we could offer, that somebody could do something for her, that we were there for her" (BE Anna F. 112-13).*

It was also explicitly stated that the husband was there as a male reference person. This was related to the aim to give Lena positive experiences of males. *"So that Lena could decide how near they were allowed to be" (KO Ms S 328).*

There were three reasons why the programme in Portugal was chosen: there was an empathetic and experienced female teacher and Fernando F. was the *"right sort of man" "Fernando is a very reserved man and can hold himself back and we thought that would be very good for Lena who found anything to do with males very frightening"*

(KO Ms S 41-44). It was also a warm country with a positive atmosphere which should counteract Lena's depressive tendencies.

The programme was not, however, able to meet Lina's therapeutic needs. *We knew that this possibility did not exist in Portugal" (KO Ms S. 78-9).* Still, this lack was outweighed by the fact that Lena had to achieve a number of other aims first before she could begin therapy. *"And that's why we felt that she should first build up her trust in other people and then with the help of these people think about therapy" (KO Ms S. 87-89).* An attempt was made in Portugal to find a therapist for Lena and a German speaking therapist was found locally. This attempt was abandoned by the care workers and the coordinator who had come to the conclusion that the therapist lacked boundaries and did not retain enough therapeutic distance. For example, after a very short time the therapist invited Lena to go and spend the weekend with her.

The location provided, through the nearby riding stables, the possibility to make contacts outside the programme. *"It was the beginning of the first relationships and friendships which were naturally very superficial, but at least a beginning" (BE Anna F. 419-20).*

4.7.2. Transition to Germany

The residential programme in Portugal concluded with a gentle transition. Lena was prepared for it over a long period of time and she was able to get to know the ambulant care worker in Germany before returning. *"And through the fact that I got to know the Care Worker Ulrike and it wasn't so abrupt, I lived in a family and then you come to Germany and suddenly you have to be a grown up" (Lena 790-1).*

"It was very helpful, because, because it happened so slowly" (Lena 793-4).

Ulrike L., the Care Worker picked up Lena and spent a little time in Portugal first, *"so, the conclusion in Portugal was, in principle very slow and gentle, because she didn't have to separate herself from the people and the country immediately"* (BE Anna F. 559 - 562). Furthermore Lena was given a dog to take with her *"a living partner, who isn't a person and isn't dangerous but is alive, who can give her something and she can give something"* (BE Anna F. 589-91).

All of the participants found the transition from the intensive care in Portugal to ambulant care in Germany to be a positive experience.

4.7.3. Ambulant after care in Germany

On her return to Germany Lena found a flat quite quickly in the middle of L. which she prepared with her Care Worker Ulrike L. Ulrike L. is a child care worker (Erzieherin) who lived near the flat and could be there quite quickly. Furthermore Ulrike L. could support Lena in many areas such as the search for a training place, coping with bureaucracy and enjoying recreational activities because she had many personal contacts and a good social network. Lena continued her training as a kindergarten teacher. After a long search for an appropriate therapist she began her first attempt at therapy. Her life skills and everyday life proceeded mostly without problems and Lena managed to complete her training and find a post as a kindergarten teacher. However, Lena restored contact to her family very quickly and was confronted again with problems in setting boundaries with the perpetrator.

Despite many attempts it proved impossible to find a suitable therapist to work with Lena on her history so that she could participate in social contacts without fear.

4.8. Participation of the young person and her parents

4.8.1. Lena's participation

Lena wasn't involved in the decision to go abroad, she was faced with a foregone conclusion and then agreed. *"Nobody asked me, somehow or so. If I wanted to go, though, in general, yes."* (Lena 156-7).

Lena could understand the decision in the sense that she had to get away from her family surroundings. It wasn't clear to her at the time why particularly Portugal and this specific Care Worker Anna F. was chosen. *"I don't know why they said, why they didn't say some other country – I couldn't understand that"* (Lena 196-7). *"but I did understand that it was too dangerous in this country and and that I couldn't go home"* (Lena 199-200). The Care Worker emphasised that it was a voluntary decision in this way:

> *"Lena took the first step by 'running away' from home and hmm, then I, at the time, B. was my coordinator, and the three of us decided, so we had, Lena and me had a good feeling about each other, the first impression was the right one"* (BE Anna F.)

The coordinator confirmed that Lena didn't participate in the decision making. *"In principle we sorted out this programme and Lena was faced with a foregone conclusion more or less and then agreed"* (KO Ms S. 58-60).In contrast, Lena had a significant influence on the design of the ambulant care programme. She decided to return to her home city, and therefore near to her family, against the advice of her Care Worker.

> *"And then I decided to go back to N. after I had a shit letter from my father (clears throat) because I thought OK .. now the good days are over and now I'm going back to Germany and it will continue exactly the same as before .. if he can find me anywhere anyway then I would prefer to go back to N. because in N. I know about hiding places I used to go where he can't find me and in K. I don't know any. .. And then I went to N."* (Lena 765-71).

4.8.2. Participation of the parents

The parents never really appeared during the entire programme. Hence, there was no involvement of the parents. Lena was already of age so their permission wasn't required. The parents weren't involved because, in order to protect Lena from her father, she had to live anonymously and this was the main reason she had to go abroad.

4.9. Quality of the relationship between the young person and the support services

4.9.1. Lena - care worker(s)

The quality of the relationship was based on three factors:

Trust

The fact that Lena was cared for for two years by the same person meant she was able to build trust for other people.

> *"with Anna I had, apart from how I felt 'in between', I had a comparatively close relationship with Anna because I could tell her stuff about what it had been like at home that I couldn't say before or hadn't said"* (Lena 343-45).

Lena told us that she hadn't said anything because she couldn't find the right words but Anna had suggested that she write them down and that's how Lena could be more open through writing letters to Anna. *"and I could write down a few situations which I hadn't been able to say before, that was important for me, to see that I, that for me it was something special because I couldn't do it before"* (Lena 350-53).

She was also able to build a trusting relationship with Fernando. *"It was very intensive for me, because .. because he was the first and also the only man, erm, where I, erm, where now, where I wasn't scared, ... that he, that impressed me, that I was there for two years and he didn't do anything to me"* (Lena 361-65).

Anna and Fernando were only able to build the much traumatised Lena's trust through closely incorporating her into their family *"or I said to her sometimes that we are very, very fond of her, that we like her very, very much"* (BE Anna F. 498-99) and despite this and at the same time, maintain a professional distance. *"Inasmuch that was a close relationship for me, but .. its very difficult, because it is often a tightrope walk, because you, because you, you can't put your finger on it, you sense the other side very clearly"* (Lena 330-32). Lena meant that she very much would have liked to be their own child. The care workers decided though that trust and honesty went together and so they reminded Lena of the reality of the situation, that the relationship was on a professional level.

"on one side she had someone at last who she could trust and on the other side she clung to them very much" (BE Anna F. 209-11). One of the biggest challenges was to maintain a balance between providing emotional support whilst remaining professional. The maintenance of this distance was at times very practical and this often led to a feeling of 'not belonging'.

"Because there was a clear separation between, 'that is my sofa as a young person and Anna and Fernando had their own sofa. I had, I had to have my own water bottle and they had other things" (Lena 304-6). *"You felt very clearly that you weren't their own child, that it was a Care Worker – young person relationship and that there was this foreign element"* (Lena 304-6).

Despite this dilemma with the problematic issue of proximity and distance on both sides it was still possible for Lena, for the first time in her life, to have a positive experience of trusting. Lena was able to have another trusting experience in her encounter with Ulrike L. the Care Worker in Germany *"If I hadn't had Ulrike then I wouldn't have managed it"* (Lena 823-4). *"and that Ulrike simply accompanied me ... that someone was there who arranged with me 'I'll pick you up from school and if your father is there, don't get in with him, because I'm there' "* (Lena 832-33).

Dependability

Lena was able to build up her trust because the Care Worker couple showed themselves as being dependable. Lena experienced a reliable and consequential togetherness, not only because of the continuity in care, without changing care workers but also in the way they behaved with each other. *"There I learnt that .. that there are people who for two years in a row always do or did what they said they would"* (Lena 272-76).

Protection and Security

For the most part, Lena felt very safe in Portugal. Initially, she was scared her father would find out where she was and would turn up at her door but Fernando in particular was able to alleviate her fears. *"And then I felt protected and I was extremely impressed that Fernando as a man [...] I'm not his child or something, that he would stand up for me"* (Lena 272 – 276).

4.9.2. Lena - coordinator

In the beginning, Lena was very critical of the Coordinator because she felt that the things that she told the Care Worker in confidence were being shared with the coordinator behind her back:

> *"And then I noticed how they rang the Coordinator Ms S and that it was always procedure that seemed to be a bit secretive"* (Lena 527-9). *"because I didn't know what they were*

telling her and never had the chance to say my side of the story and I don't know what they said and I don't want to Ms S. to think about me in a way that wasn't true" (Lena 533-6).

This changed over time as *"she [rem: the coordinator] took on a central and important role"* (Lena 541-2). The coordinator became a central figure who was always responsible for Lena. She also remained as a constant at the partly painful leave from her care workers in Portugal as Lena mentioned at different times in her interview:

"Ms S was just as important for me as Portugal in a way" (Lena 504-5) *"for me she was the one who- that sounds so stupid now – but she, she, saved me* (Lena 545-6). *"and because of that, I think in this whole Portugal thing, she is the most important person, because I had the feeling that she was yet another layer of protection for me"* (Lena 548-52). *"her visits were something special for me or important for me because she .. for me she is, the one who protected me. Yes"* (Lena 558-60).

The arduously achieved trust in adults was maintained because she remained in contact with her until the present day.

"but at the same time too, regardless how often they tell me, even when Ms S or Ulrike, Anna or Fernando tell me a hundred times that as long as I want contact they will stay in contact with me and that it's important for them, I don't really believe it, because I am so scared that it's all over" (Lena 922-25).

Keeping the contact alive was very important for Lena because that was the only way to compensate for her fears of abandonment and in some way, to make up for her lack of basic sense of trust.

4.10. Process design between young person and the support services

4.10.1. Social behaviour

The subject of trust was a very delicate point for Lena and also her biggest challenge. It was achieved through careful and ongoing work through the continuity in the behaviour of the Care workers in every area of life and needed to be confirmed every day.

> *"So, they were always there and they managed through the same, that was same daily routine … to show this thread of a completely normal family life, and to gain trust"* (KO Ms S 320-24).

Lena confirmed that this was the same with the ambulant care. The Care Worker stood by Lena's side in every problematic situation. For example, despite a lack of sufficient care hours, Ulrike spent many nights in the flat with Lena to help her to be able to stay in a closed room.

> *"That means, as we found out that Lena went out at night Ulrike said spontaneously: 'I don't care whether this is an am-*

bulant care or not, I'll stay here with you .. at night. And then she stayed for nights" (KO Ms S. 376-79).

Lena was also able to have positive experiences in relationships, especially with men through Fernando's dependable and empathetic manners and behaviour.

4.10.2. Emotional maturity

Lena and her care workers noticed that she didn't know and couldn't do many everyday things. This formed an important part of her care so that there was always someone who looked after her and was able to practice her life skills through repetition. Today Lena values this a lot.

> *"they took the time to explain 20 million times how to hold a fork or how to tie shoelaces [...] which I had always been able to hide, nobody had noticed before but Anna noticed"* (Lena 277-9, 281-3).

Or she learnt that *"that you can get a plaster if you have hurt yourself"* (Lena 234-5). Lena gradually learnt to be independent through these valuable repetitions and support.

> *"there were many areas of life where you noticed quickly that she got stuck in her development as small child and that you needed an improbable amount of time to bring her up to a level"* (BE Anna F. 160-3).

The care workers were able to negotiate the ongoing tightrope walk between allowing Lena to have regressive phases and encouraging her to behave in in an age appropriate way. The setting was suitable to support the development of her emotional maturity and have new therapeutic learning experiences.

> "My niece was visiting and left her sandpit toys behind … and the toys were lying on a gravel mound and … there was Lena with the toys and … and Lena was playing with them for at least for two hours" (BE Anna F. 236-9).
>
> "I noticed that a large part of her childhood, including her time as an infant was missing, .. for several weeks I read her bedtime stories sitting on her bed [laughs] like you do it as, yes a mother" (BE Anna F. 331-33).

It was possible to reach an age appropriate level of independence including the emotional maturity. *"They were all things that she learnt little by little, that made her very proud"* (BE Anna F. 234-5).

4.10.3. Family relationships

Lena rated being protected from her father very highly. *"Yeah, that they're taking care of me, like … yeah, they took care of me, you know, and protected me like nobody else had in the past and .. and that contributed a bit to me .. feeling safer."* In the beginning, she was scared her father would find her and be at the door but Anna was able to take away her fear.

> *"Well, she sort of role played the scenario and said 'Yes, when, ah, my father is at the door, I wouldn't open the door anyway, they would open the door and I would stand way behind them and Anna would stand in front of me and then Fernando would stand in front of Anna and regardless of what my father would do they wouldn't let him get round them to get to me and Fernando would fight with my father to stop him getting to me"* (Lena 261-7).

In Portugal Lena wrote repeated letters to the care workers and herself, pretending to be her father but this was unmasked which was a milestone in the programme.

> *"that was a massive issue, the whole thing, letters kept being pushed under the door with violent threats, but luckily we resolved that sympathetically and then we could move on to the next phase"* (BE Anna F. 311-4).

Despite this, her problems in establishing boundaries with her father could only be partially resolved in both Portugal and Germany. Lena decided for herself to return to N. where her father lived nearby and she reported that everything had started again. *"I would say that the programme always pivoted around this repetition of what happened in the past"* (KO Ms S. 262-4).

While in ambulant care in Germany, Lena had to rely mostly on herself with regard to protection. Ulrike L. the Care Worker was able to offer Lena a few ways of helping in that she organised transport to school where Lena's father liked to wait for her. But she couldn't forbid this contact.

"That was all still up in the air, I was still scared shitless of my father and stupidly I still reacted to him and made contact again and then .. just like before Portugal it went on again, although not so bad because I wasn't living at home anymore but he always intercepted me everywhere even in front of the school" (Lena 818 -823).

4.10.4. Life skills

The everyday life skills like school, training, hygiene and structuring her day were mostly without disturbance but in contrast, those things that are usually are taken for granted like which clothes were appropriate for the weather, appropriate behaviour when in pain or injured or knowledge of everyday routines (eating with cutlery, tying shoelaces etc.) were integrated into the care process to help her mature as a person.

Another central aim of the programme was to help Lena develop the competencies required for making and keeping social contacts. In Portugal it was the riding stables, which provided this opportunity and she was encouraged to go by the Care Worker but found it very difficult.

"She wanted to be with me all of the time but that isn't possible, life isn't like that, you have to take the blinkers off sometimes and meet new people. She got to know Elke, for example and got on well with her" (BE Anna F. 250-54).

"Mmm, I think that the riding thing was good for Lena, although she never actually rode at the stables [laugh] but did some of the grooming, and entered into the first relationships,

friendships, that were naturally very superficial but at least a start" (BE Anna F. 417-20).

In Germany personal interests were developed like, for example a drum course, which she is still attending today.

The trust which Lena was able to gain with the care workers in the programme played an important role in her development of life skills. It meant that Lena was able to put aside her extreme shyness and anxiousness to the extent that she was able to live more independently and find and keep a work place and the necessary social contacts that they required. Ulrike L. had a very pragmatic approach. She did what needed doing to move along this process. *"so, whether it was something formal, whether it was about finances, applications and so on, as well as visiting the therapist, she prepared incredibly well and supported and accompanied Lena"* (KO Ms S. 405-8).

4.11. Stakeholder collaboration

Anna F. valued the collaboration with the Coordinator as helpful and open. *"When I had problems I always had the feeling that the coordinator Ms S. was listening (BE Anna F. 525-6). I always felt very well that I was in good hands, always"* (BE Anna F. 530). Both Anna and the Coordinator had a negative rating for the work with the therapist in Portugal. This was because they felt that the therapist didn't maintain the necessary professional distance. For this reason the therapy was terminated early by the care workers.

The Coordinator rated the work with the care workers in Portugal and in Germany as good *"Basically the teamwork was very good, very open, can be characterised as very good. This was the case in both locations, I had a high level of trust and openness" (Ms S. 423-25).*

4.12. Conclusion of the programme and ongoing support

The project was concluded in a gentle way with reducing care hours when Lena was 23 years old. The Coordinator remembers it as a successful outcome which achieved the support plan goals:

"So Lena had all of the tools she needed, she knows who she can turn to and now needs to move on from her history. She is able to manage her life or when a relapse is triggered she then knows who to turn to in order to find help (KO Ms S. 524-538).

What remained was a need for further therapy which Lena, with the new experience she had gained, had to organise herself.

4.13. The impact of the support and its effects as seen by the interviewees

Today, Lena sees a direct connection between the two phases of her programme and her current stage of development:

"I think that, if I were to answer spontaneously, I would say that everything that I can do now, I learnt in Portugal (Lena 980-1) *"but if the period of support in Germany from Ulrike hadn't happened, if things had continued in the way they did before Portugal then I wouldn't even have been able to get a flat for myself"* (Lena 860-3).

4.13.1. Social behaviour

Lena made it clear in her interview that she still feels very unsure in her day to day life and of other people despite the experiences she had in building trust in relationships in Portugal and Germany which was necessary for her survival. She clearly described the limitations of her learning in the programme:

"I notice in everyday life .. that I am different from other people of my age. Compared to other people, I have learnt lots of strategies to hide things from others but I still have lots of things that aren't normal and that draw attention to me and that's difficult because my behaviour draws attention and prevents me from doing things" (Lena 846-50).

Lena still feels anxious with strangers who she meets at work or privately and with whom she has occasional and superficial relationships, she still has the old fears and suffers under the *"inability to build trust with any stranger"* (Lena 964). At the time of the interview, she appeared to have little hope that she would ever be able to conquer this fear:

> *"I couldn't really believe and I don't think I do believe that trust won't always be an issue, because I am just as mistrustful and just as cautious and aware as I was before Portugal"* (Lena 1016-19).

This shows the limitations of the social educational work and Lena's need for therapy is still very strong. But the coordinator who still has sporadic contact with Lena drew attention to the fact that Lena also made a little progress towards the end of the programme.

> *"Yes, she could be more open, more open to other people. She has managed to communicate with other people and sometimes to do things with people of the same age for example. She wouldn't have been able to do this at all before the programme"* (KO Ms S. 536-38). And further *"Yes, meanwhile she ... could maintain social contacts a little"* (KO Ms S. 561).

With regard to Lena's previously fear filled relationship to men, the Care Worker in Portugal noted towards the end of her stay:

> *"I think too that her view of men has been extended somewhat [...] perhaps she now realises that not all men are brutal and not all men are the same as her father"* BE Anna F. 353-56).
>
> *"The big step at the end of the programme was that she was able to ride pillion on Fernando's motorbike or be alone with him in his car – and she wasn't scared."* (BE Anna F. 353 – 356)

Lena mentioned this after a recent contact with the care workers in Portugal *"and that for me Fernando was very special [...] where I, where we greeted each other he used to look at me and he embraced me and I noticed that I wasn't scared"* (Lena 388-92).

The reunion between Anna, Klaus and Lena after seven years left a lasting impression with Anna: *"and the first thing I noticed was that Lena wasn't so stooped and withdrawn as she had been ... in her body language she stood up with straight shoulders, they were, it was great"* (BE Anna F. 398-401).

Anna F was obviously surprised at how Lena had developed in the meantime and was very happy *"to see how she had turned into an amazing, attractive woman with both feet firmly on the ground"* (BE Anna F. 684-5).

Anna F. rated Lena's experience *"that she [...] saw that there are people who don't close their eyes with regard to her past, who don't say I don't see that so I don't have to do anything"* (BE Anna F. 647-9) as important.. Anna still hopes that Lena will find an appropriate therapy so that she can achieve a satisfactory quality of life.

4.13.2. Emotional maturity

Lena now has a feeling of strength and stability as a result of the patient care of the workers in Portugal. They accompanied her through a learning process which allowed her to catch up on the everyday skills that she would normally have learnt as a small child.

"Even now in Germany .. it gives me strength to know what I can do, what I learnt there and that keeps me upright" (Lena 382-84) or *" that, mostly it stayed with me because I was there

for two years and it is a treasure, that I described earlier, that means a tremendous amount to me and that I, even though six years have passed, that naturally these experiences that I had there are still with me" (Lena 416-20).

This is confirmed by Anna *"Mm, the first thing is that she can now manage practical things much better, like the issues with tying shoelaces and eating"* (BE Anna F. 645-6). Now Lena has more insight and can contrast her experiences in Portugal with those in her birth family and it enables her to see what is 'normal'.

"On the whole I think that I noticed this difference between what I learnt at home and .. or what I did because I hadn't learnt and what it should normally be like" (Lena 1022-25).

4.13.3. Family relationships

The care and support teams all agreed that a social educational approach to deal with the family dynamic reached its limits. At least it achieved the point that by the end of the ambulant care, according to Lena, she had been able to break off the very stressful contact to her family *"that, that somehow we managed to stop it [Lena being waylaid by her father in front of her school in N. Author's note]* (Lena 836).

The one thing that Lena hasn't managed to achieve, according to the coordinator, was to be open with professionals about what happened to her.

"Anyway, she couldn't open herself, she didn't manage to do that, with therapists and so on but as I've said, she could

share some of her experiences with the people who know her history, ... she gained a bit of security and self-confidence, that she had something. Anyway at least she managed to completely break her contact with her family" (KO Ms S. 543-49).

Lena tried several therapists which turned out to be very tedious and still didn't have the outcome she wanted.

"When I started therapy in Germany after I got back ... but, without exaggerating, I needed a whole year before I could even sit in the same room and answer questions about what happened at home, I could only nod, so that I needed a year even before they had any idea what the issues were". (Lena 704-9)

4.13.4. Life skills

Lena reported that there were still lots of difficulties in relationship with strangers but that in Portugal she had partly found a way to control her fear in social situations. Her situation at the end of the programme was as follows:

Lena completed her training as a kindergarten teacher and went on to the probationary year in a kindergarten. She lived in her own flat and was in therapy, although it hadn't had the effect she hoped for. Lena was able to have contact with strangers within a professional context and was able to deal with financial and bureaucratic things independently. By the end of the programme, according to Lena, her contact with her family, respectively her father had ended.

At the time of the interview Lena had a permanent job as kindergarten teacher and had, in parallel begun an accompanying course of studies as a social worker. Lena would like to move away from her current career as kindergarten teacher to work as an adviser which is why she had the ambition to study.

4.14. Lena's ideas for her future

Lena is very hard working and inquisitive *"Yes I want to do well in my studies"* (Lena 935). *"anyway I know that there I want to learn a lot and that I'm very thirsty for knowledge [...] that lots of things interest me and so on and that I enjoy learning"* (Lena 949, 951-952). She wishes very much to be able to

> *"manage it, that I, that I don't attract attention like a normal person, that I can sleep in my flat like a normal person, that I can behave so I don't stick out, that I, that I carry on working on myself, that I can stay in the flat and that I don't always have to be on my guard in everyday life. I would like to change that but I don't know how yet, because of this problem I probably need therapy but I can't speak or build up trust to some strange person"* (Lena 956-64).

4.15. Summary

The reconstruction of Lena's case study and the analysis of the interviews show that for young people who have experienced severe trauma, a social educational programme is not in itself enough to have a positive effect on significantly psychiatric disorders in the long term.

On the other hand, for a young person in this situation with a high need for therapy the pedagogic element is also very important to deal with their issues. For Lena the first priority was protection from her family and trust building measures and this was more important in the first instance than therapy. This was because Lena couldn't even begin therapy before she was able to place her trust in a stranger. The participation in a programme was then the right decision. It would have been better if Lena had been able to begin her therapy whilst in Portugal. It would have been very desirable to have the necessary therapeutic capacity within the programme in order to enable Lena to deal with her past and develop her emotional maturity.

The untiring availability of the care workers and their high level of empathy in the way they engaged with Lena were beneficial during the two phases of the programme. They were able to adapt their work according to the level of progress that Lena made. This was the reason that Lena was able to engage at all with other people in a social and work context. Lena and the care workers confirm that the experiences she had with the four care workers led to this improvement. The intensity and length of the programme were beneficial even if it wasn't possible to meet her therapeutic needs.

The transition from the residential programme in Portugal to the ambulant care in Germany was especially successful. It was important that Lena, who has always found it hard to relate to strangers, could get to know the Ulrike F. in Portugal prior to leaving as she was able to go on to develop a close relationship with her. Thus she did not see the end of the programme as abrupt. Therefore it was possible for Lena to develop a new contact and trust to an additional person in a safe and protected environment in Portugal.

One can't be sure whether, if Lena had followed her care workers advice and returned to a different place in Germany, would have been better from a therapeutic point of view. However it might have been better if Lena had been able to avoid the disturbances caused by her father on her return to Germany.

It is noteworthy that all of the workers were closely agreed about the perceived positive outcomes as well as the limitations of the programme.

5. Conclusion

5.1. The caring relationship as foundation and opportunity

It became clear in the case studies that the caring relationship is the most important element in the provision of individual social learning opportunities. This isn't a new discovery: In pedagogic and psychological literature the type of relationship between the care worker and the (mostly traumatised and mistrustful) children and young people has always been seen as a significant, even the <u>most</u> significant factor for the success of an intervention.

Klawe says *"the personality of the carer, their social competences, their attitudes and social network"* are the most important factors for *"successful progress and outcomes of the caring process"*[16]

Fröhlich-Gildhoff, in a study of 1:1 care in youth welfare says that the variables of acceptance, trust, empathy, persistence, honesty and clarity in the attitude of carers are important constituents of a carer's personality. In addition, he describes six central and essential elements in the form of the caring relationship: practical help/support, being there and accessibility, providing challenges and confrontation, setting boundaries, encouragement and trust as well as fun. [17]

All of these elements are present in the cross section of case studies which were evaluated as part of this research[18]. As can be expected, the individual care processes and contributory factors de-

---

16 Klawe 2010: 17

17 Fröhlich-Gildhoff 2003: 32

18 vgl. Riemann (2012):

scribed in this research present a very differentiated picture of the quality of each of the relationships and the elements leading to a positive relationship.

As a result of Lena's history and her fear and insecurity both phases of her programme placed a lot of emphasis on care which promoted trust, protection and security as well as including practical help and offers of support. Lena mentions often that the continual presence and absolute dependability of the care workers was very important to her.

For André, with his destructive tendencies and antisocial behaviour, the important elements were challenge and confrontation as well as the setting of boundaries and practical everyday support – and at the same time he needed emotional support, familiarity and almost constant accessibility to his Carer.

Clearly the range of different requirements in the pedagogic work also requires a range of different carer personalities to provide real help in the young person's development which complement their individual characters, skills, and experience and so on.

With regard to establishing the best fit between young person and carer we refer to the relevant attachment theories and requirements established through research for the development of supportive, encouraging and healing relationships with the Carer.

To return to the value of the activities based on relationships which have been evaluated in this research, the comments by the interviewees with regard to relationships have generated the following main features:

1. be authentic, predictable and consistent
2. be dependable and committed
3. be persistent, be there and remain there

4. acknowledge, respect and value
5. be emotionally and physically available
6. challenge and confront
7. set boundaries and de-escalate
8. support and accompany
9. do things together and have fun
10. show all facets of yourself, not only the professional side
11. be a role model (father/mother and friend)

This list is in accordance with the characteristics described by Fröhlich-Gildhoff (1 to 9) although the difference between the way care workers approached the young people and the way they acted is not drawn out in this research because the interviewees focused more on what happened (what happened during the programme, what did they do together, what was in hindsight helpful etc).

The only differences are that our research identifies the additional elements of 'show all facets of yourself, not only the professional side' and 'being a role model' as being valuable. This finding is more closely examined in the following paragraphs.

The personal elements in 1:1 care

The case studies do not provide a simple answer to the question as to whether there is a "perfect balance between personal and professional involvement"[19] in residential and ambulant individual pedagogic care. All of the case studies that we evaluated show that, in the opinion of the interviewees a helpful care relationship is decidedly more than just a professional relationship for a certain amount of time *"for*

---
19 Baierl 2010: 66

which the pedagogue is paid and which he would usually not commit to privately given similar circumstances" [20]

This does not only apply to care programmes in which the care workers (and in some cases their families) live with the young person but it also applies to ambulant care situations. After long discussions, the research team reached the following conclusion:

The "personal component" seems to be an essential and deciding ingredient in working with youth whose previous lives had been majorly influenced by trauma and abandonment. The next few paragraphs will serve to illustrate this point.

Young People long for a sense of normality and to belong

In the stories of the young persons, we find descriptions indicative of a yearning for something that is seen as normal and apparently the embodiment of an ideal family.

The 28 year old Lena describes a situation in the car where she was cold and asked her care worker whether she could borrow her jacket. She was obviously not sure whether the care worker would agree but asked in the hope the care worker would respond in the way a "normal" family member would. The jacket was a symbol of nearness, safety, security and the feeling of being at home:

> "[...] and erm, she let me (put it on) and said that I could cover myself with it and that made, erm …yes, it made me feel good because, erm … I don't know, it's this concern again, that

---

[20] ibid: 65

she, that she did it, although it was her jacket [...] and there were a lot of situations where I had the feeling that I was at home and that I belong" (Lena).

André remembers a situation where he went on holiday with his Care Worker, he was very thankful, and still couldn't quite believe it. A break in everyday life, the opportunity to have some time away, to spend some time together and to share a moment of peace – the same as a family holiday which André had probably never experienced before.

"it was like this, Ms O. and me, she just thought, let's just go to Denmark and have a holiday, yes ... for a whole week. That was a really nice time with her .. [...]" (André).

Christian, according to what he said, experienced a family atmosphere in Italy that he probably never had at home:
"What I really enjoyed was, erm, that basically it was a family atmosphere ... anyway, erm, one had, .. I seldom had the feeling that I was being 'cared' for, I can remember that really well.. " (Christian)

The care relationship as an opportunity for maturing emotionally

The longing for normality includes things that did not happen sufficiently in life before the individual social care programme and which need to be made up for. So there are situations which occur during the programme which on the surface have little to do with pedagogy but which prove their therapeutic potential in that they nurture emotional development in the young person.

So as in the story of the pacifier André where was allowed to relive his 'babyhood' which, according to the Care Worker, made it possible for him to move on to further personal development. It wasn't only important for him to be allowed, as a teenager, to walk around with a pacifier in his mouth but that the Care Worker was not judgemental either. The Carer saw André's need and responded to it regardless of what it looked like and this enabled the young person to become more emotionally mature.

Or there are the examples of 19-year-old Lena who was able to play with sandpit toys and had bedtime stories read to her and 16-year-old Christian who made wooden swords and played with them which was only possible when he was accompanied by a care worker in an isolated place in Italy.

The relevance and importance of relationships in the view of the Young People

The authors were surprised that five of the young people involved in the research said that the Mother/Father role or the Mate-role of the Carer was a central aspect and was valued. André and Christian said the following:

> "[...] and the MS O. was like that, .. she was almost like a mother, almost. Anyway she took me home with her and .. she had a few things, she really supported me just like Mr M. But she was a woman and that was a bit different to Mr M." (André).

"[...] I'd say I got myself together in Italy, that .. was simply because ... the care from Klaus B., who was my personal Care Worker and the programme leader, .. we are still friends today, we spoke on the phone yesterday, the influence that Klaus had on me .. was large ... he, basically, yes, on one side .. one has to say .. was almost a father figure" (Christian).

It is often difficult to differentiate between the care relationship in an individual social educational programme and a parent – child relationship or friendship. Amongst other things Mother, Father and Friends are very important in the perception of the young person. They stand for empathy, security, guidance, care, trust and dependability. These are all attributes that are essential for a successful programme. This is particularly true of individual social educational care that, in part involves the private lives of care workers and where there can be a very fuzzy line between this and the father/mother/friend role.

In relation to this, Pollak talks about the sometimes contradictory dual nature of the relationship between carer and cared for which he separates into the specific and a diffuse aspect of the relationship.

The specific aspect is a formal and professional role which is based on theoretical expertise. However the more diffuse aspect of the relationship is based more on an extremely robust and affective bond as well as building and maintaining trust which isn't tied to standard criteria but is more akin to a primary social relationship like a parent or friend.[21] This contradictory and dual character and the time limited nature of the programme can be experienced as difficult and ambiva-

---

21   Pollak 2002: in Klawe 2010: 339f.

lent by the young people. Lena expressed her perception and feelings in the following way:

> "[...] inasmuch it was very close, our relationship but ... that was so difficult, because it is often a balancing act [...] you are only the young person and you know they are being paid to do it and you know that you ... that everything you are hoping for, that you, yes that you can stay there for ever and [embarrassed laugh] all this stuff and everything, you know that that is only wishful thinking, and then you are woken up ..." (Lena).

The danger of over-involvement – or near is only good with distance...

The question of the diffuse aspect of the relationships was not only important for all of the young people in the case studies. The reports of the Care Workers, the Coordinators and the Case Workers from the Youth Welfare Offices demonstrated that in both residential and ambulant 1:1 care measures there was a level of engagement by the Carer Workers which went way beyond what they were paid for and what they were able to cope with at times. Yet, it was this intensity of their involvement which was perceived as being a significant driver in the development of the programmes. It is also interesting that at the time the interviews took place, the contact between all of the young people and their ex-carers continued at least sporadically.

The authors of this research regard a strong personal component in the caring relationship as a significant success factor for the social educational programmes with traumatised young people.

There is of course a danger in over-involvement in the caring relationship and, with justification Baierl warns of not maintaining a clear distinction between personal and professional level. [22]

This is the impression, for example, in Christian's ambulant care. This was the first time that the Care Worker had done this work. She reports the very high levels of stress as a result of Christians challenging behaviour. She describes it as *"a long and endless crisis"*. On reading her description the question arises as to how she could put up with the young man for such a long time and to what extent she was clear about her role. There is no evidence from the interviews that there was any continuity in providing her with professional supervision.

Our question is not so much <u>whether</u> these caring relationships should contain a personal element but how far it is possible to recognise the special character of this work with its systemic ambivalence and to reflect the relationship (together with the young person and their family), to provide professional support and to provide adequate professional supervision for the Care Worker. These considerations should form part of a range of standards that define what good quality individual social education is.

5.2. Working with biographies

With today's knowledge, working with biographies should be a self-evident part of the repertoire of methodologies used in intensive social educational care settings because trauma and emotional deficits are common in the care of these young people.

22

In the interviews there are a range of reflections by the care workers and the Coordinators which show that biography is a very important element, in their view.

A focus of their reflections is the support of the young people in their search for their place in the family – which was a source of sometimes extreme conflict in all of the young people and had different outcomes with each of them: Both André und Christian succeeded in getting closer to their father or mother. Other young people hadn't succeeded sufficiently in achieving reconciliation with reality and to return to establish their place in the family at the time of the interviews.

However, it is mostly unclear to what extent specific methods were used in working with these biographies.

It is also not clear from the material in the interviews whether and to what degree working with biography with the young people was explicit, whether it was intrinsic and concomitant or whether it was secondary consideration. It appears that little work was done with André on grieving for his mother who died from a severe illness when he was very young. In the programme with Christian, discussion about his father was to a great extent taboo.

During the evaluation of the material and group discussions amongst the team the question was raised as to how far - for example with Lena or Christian – the trauma in their biography indicated the need for a therapeutic intervention. In contrast, some other young people who have had a long career in youth welfare and psychiatric hospitals and who are then placed in intensive one to one social education care, usually require stabilisation by their care workers first if any further therapeutic intervention is to be successful. Finally we can assume that the 1:1 Carers also provide therapeutic interventions without necessarily knowing that they did (see the chapter "Care as an opportunity for developing emotional maturity").

As a result of these considerations we come to the following conclusions for provider organisations:

- All staff in the organisation should be trained in the use of biography in their work. Two particular methods should be considered: The Timeline and the Genogram (rem: also known as a McGoldrick-Gerson study, a Lapidus Schematic or a Family Diagram) with a focus on family resources. Additionally, it is recommended that the young people keep 'life books' or 'memory boxes' which document their life stories before and during the care programme . In house training should be provided to ensure that this and other creative methods are used. Alternatively the knowledge about these methods could be passed on by coordinators.
- Coordinators should be trained in the use of attachment theory and trauma pedagogic so that they have the tools to advise and supervise other staff.

5.3. Support plans versus themes

The regulations in Germany (SGB VIII) require that before and during a programme a support plan and support aims are to be prepared.

The case studies show that there is often a discrepancy between these aims and the themes that arise during the delivery of the programme.

The formulation of the aims is guided in the main by important long term goals which consist mostly of practical achievements such as completing education or training, improving social skills and similar guidance. Problematic social behaviour or the themes that arise as the result of a difficult life such as emotional immaturity or relationship with family are not often mentioned or only very generally referred to in passing. In reality and as a rule, the development of an emotional foundation and willingness to participate is necessary in order to achieve these long term goals.

Lena, according to all of the participants, couldn't deal with her age related themes (she joined the programme in Italy at the age of 18) in the first few months. The first things she had to learn and be nurtured in were feeling safe, life skills and develop trust for the adult carers, in particular the male carer.

The research team developed the hypothesis that Christian was only able to deal with the subject of education when the Care Worker in Italy took his own preoccupations and thoughts seriously and he didn't need to use all of his energy to be threatening and everything that went with it.

For André the idea of going to school or developing a training plan was out of the question during the programme. The first priority for the care workers was to develop a connection at all and to strengthen the family so that André could develop a relationship with them again. If these more important needs and challenges are not recognised and identified in the support plan it can lead to a false view: The formal and unachievable goals act as a way of measuring success and the tedious day to day work of the Carers on the often existential needs of the young person is in danger of being devalued. This perceived deficit then often has an impact on the available advance information, medical history and progress reports and probably isn't conducive to the collaborative work between young person and carer.

A comparison of the analysis of the main themes in the case studies and the expressed goals described in the support plans shows that the method of developing support plans needs reviewing. While listing important and objective long term goals is important, it is desirable to place greater emphasis on developing and formulating individual needs to enable a more appropriate allocation of resources to support the carers in their work.

This research, based on a number of interviews and documents has generated a number of topics that can be used to categorise this approach. The categories include:

- Emotional maturity
- Family relationships
- Social behaviour
- Life skills

5.4. Participation

5.4.1. Participation of the young people

Child welfare is not the same as child's will.[23] This simple truth is mentioned in some of these Case Studies in some way by the young people themselves. So how far is participation by young people in the decision making process possible or sensible? How far can and should

---

23 vgl. Dettenborn 2010: 82 ff.

the opinion of the young person be taken into account when the type of programme, its conclusion or location is chosen?

It is clear from the case studies that, at the beginning of the programme, the young people involved were in crisis which means that real participation in the choice of programme is not the most important thing. Lena was primarily concerned with protection and there appeared to be no alternative to the programme offered by the Youth Welfare Office and the programme providers in Portugal. Christian and André however remember that to begin with they were not very motivated and had little guidance with regard to the programmes offered. The 21-year-old André described the then 15-year-old André as not being "mature enough" to be involved in the planning of the programme. Christian records that he doesn't even know how he even ended up in the emergency shelter, whether it was decided by someone else or if he made the decision. Especially here it is important to make the process as transparent as possible, to get them involved and show that they are taken seriously.

In individual cases and in an effort to take the young person's participation seriously, the services go with the decision of the young person which appears to be more of an attempt to follow the child's will and not their welfare. Christian, for example, initially refused all offers of help so it was not possible to involve him in the decision making in the sense described above.

The consequence was that he landed on the street again and again and had to have ambulant care there. This existential experience was what probably first made it possible to move on to a productive way of working.

When the will and the welfare of the child contradict each other and the child's will is put in first place, it is essential that from the pedagogic point of view, there is close support available in the resulting care programme. At the age of 18 as he achieved adulthood, Christian decided to conclude his programme in Italy and return to Germany against the wishes of the service provider and the Youth Welfare Office. Today, at the age of 26 Christian says that this was a biggest mistake of his life. In particular he criticised the limited amount of ambulant support available to him when he returned.

In contrast to Christian, Lena was supported in this process in a way which met her needs. Lena decided, against the advice of the service provider, to return to her home city. She received the support which met her needs and with their help negotiated the return to Germany successfully so that the support could be concluded 16 months later.

Participation is then a sort of real involvement by the young person in the sense that they can decide how their programme continues. Participation should be an inherent and long term part of the structure of the relationship and the programme. This requires a high level of transparency and consistency on the part of the service provider and the care workers so that the young person is always clear about the individual steps. Participation is therefore more than just the offering of alternatives, it is the involvement of the child's will in its totality; a joint enterprise in action, reflection, exploration of wishes, expectations, motivation and goals.

Being seen and taken seriously within the relationship between the young person and Carer plays an important role in stabilising the young person and therefore their self efficacy. In the interviews the young people continually emphasised how important it was to be taken seriously by the Care Worker and how significant an element it was in the structure of the relationship.

5.4.2. Participation by the parents

The analysis of the case studies implied that the service providers were relieved when parents, at the very least, did not place obstacles in the path of delivering the care programme. Participation by parents was often confined to formal activities [rem: like signing off on paperwork] (André, Christian) or played no role (Lena) and only in rare cases there was participation in its widest sense.

There was little opportunity for participation by the parents as they were seldom present.

It is not possible to see from the case studies what attitude was taken to the parents as part of the care work in the sense that parents were considered to be part of the care programme.

The following points can be made from the point of view of their participation in support of successful programme:

1. participation of the young person is particularly important in the transition phases like changing locations, beginning and end of a programme, departure etc.
2. Young people should be involved to the degree which their own personal development and situation at the beginning of the programme allows. This requires transparency and communication.
3. Participation is a continuous process and can take place in a deepening relationship. It is an important foundation to enable the young person to experience more s self efficacy. There must be corresponding and sensitive development of the relationship which encourages attachment behaviour.
4. Participation also involves going with the wishes of the young person which might appear to contradict the objective

expectations of the Carer. This requires good support moving forward.
5. Participation by parents should be more than just taking them into account in formal processes. It is preferable that the carers attitude is that parents are seen as a resource. Working with parents as such should be more comprehensive and integrated into the care process as a matter of course.

5.5. Resources and potential

5.5.1. The young person's resources

Making use of the resources and potential of the young people in the pedagogic work means firstly looking carefully at the characteristics, capabilities, attitudes, value base, interest and goals of the young person and valuing them. They should be included in the work and developed, opening new avenues to try things out and discover new things.

In the English publication, the chosen case studies show that the care workers had a good eye for identifying resources, in particular with Christian. With Lena it was possible to use her existing cognitive resources and with André it was above all his social skills.

At the same time, the search for resources requires looking for potential: Lena was encouraged by the care workers in Portugal to visit a riding stables regularly. It was not the work with horses which was most important but the opportunity to mix with young people of the same age. This was something that Lena would not have been able to do by herself. With Christian it was the opportunity to undertake work placements which eventually woke his interest in jewellery making.

It should be of concern to pedagogues in intensive social education 1:1 Care to ensure that they look beyond the existing inclinations and talents and provide a varied offer to allow the opportunity to have new experiences and develop new resources.

It is often the case that Young People in 1:1 care have not learnt to make use of their existing creative potential so that they are available for others. In addition the ability to reflect on how their behaviour affects others is under developed in many of the young people. In the German version this strength is only seen in four of the seven case studies. One of the tasks of the care worker is then to 'reframe' the destructive characteristics they exhibit and place them in a strengthened, new and positively framed context. The intention of giving the young people this kind of feedback is to help them achieve a change of perspective.

In this research Christian is a particularly good example: The care worker in Italy was the most successful in recognising the interests, themes and behaviour that the young man had to date offered the world as resources that needed to be freed from their biographical 'crust'. In the numberless discussions on the themes of philosophy, literature and art, it was possible to help Christian find a way to tap into his diverse cognitive resources and later to discover a potential in craftsmanship.

5.5.2. Family resources

Finally we should look at the resources that might be available from parents, siblings, grandparents and so on to recognise them and make them available, especially with regard to children.

The three case studies in the English publication provide sobering news: According to the care workers of all three young people, family resources are a scarce commodity. Both André und Christian grew up in single parent families as a result of divorce or death and so not even present in memories. Both had (step)parents who suffered from substance abuse or psychiatric illness or were unable to cope with bringing their children up and were therefore not available. Lena's mother didn't appear at all and her father probably mostly through restaging her experiences. For Christian the only significant attachment figure mentioned was his grandmother.

It could be argued that the structures and resources required to undertake ongoing and comprehensive work with parents (in order to integrate their resources into the intensive social education programme) do not exist. At the same time the authors hold the view that the professionals should take the stance that they should remain open to working with the family, in which ever form is relevant, and leave enough room in the intensive social educational care programme for this work. This is of particular significance because, as these case studies show, with the exception of Lena (whose father who was accused of serious abuse) the subject of "my place in the family" was one which the young people wanted to process.

The following interventions which aim to strengthen and involve family resources are mentioned by the professionals involved:

- Making and maintaining contact between the young person and their parents and de-escalation if necessary (André, Christian)
- Reflexion with the young people over their needs, wishes,

longing and expectations in relation to their parents, a reality check with young people as to what their parents can do for them and what not? (Christian)
- Relive attachment relevant behaviour - particularly in conflict situations, with the care workers. Find ways to develop new behaviour patterns so that a new relationship experiences with the parents are possible (André, Christian)
- Accompanied parent visits in the programme location
- Mediation and "family circles"
- Parent training at Jugendhilfe Phöinix e. V
- Explicit work with parents in the form of meetings with the parents

(the last four interventions can be found in the original German publication)

The impact of successful work with parents:
André and Christian were supported in developing a new relationship with their father (André) and mother (Christian). Although both the mother (Andre) and father(Christian) are still taboo to some extent.

A former young adult has continued to come to terms with the reality of the relationship with her parents after the programme by herself and had to relinquish a whole range of hopes and wishes. There is, however, a tendency towards role change in dealing with her father who is an alcoholic.

A Young Person rejects contact with their mother after failed attempts at initiating it and passes this attitude on to her daughter. There is no contact to the father either.

A young person who had spent 10 years in intensive social education still lives with his mother who developed enormously during the programme but he refuses contact to his father, (probably out of loyalty to his mother).

Another young person had always longed for the recognition and love of his father but only ever received practical support. The mother, as a result of her own addiction to alcohol, was unable to provide support either during or after the programme.

After discussions about the outcomes from the case studies, the research team are of the view that some of the following interventions and principles would have been helpful:

- A strong focus on identifying additional resources in the work with the young person and their parents and the skill to recognise and use the creative potential in apparently destructive behaviour.
- To give the Young person room to try things out and to be open for self-development so that their horizons can be opened and they acquire new knowledge and develop new skills.
- Parental work through other professionals (to make them more aware of the needs of their children)
- being more realistic about the role of the father or mother – taking into account the role(s) of the care worker(s), coregulation; at times, this might include a more challenging, proactive approach in regard to competition between parent and care worker
- Building on positive experiences between the young person and their parents in the care process and in the work with the parents
- reduce the taboo on absent parents
- Close involvement of other important reference persons (e.g. grandmother, sister)

5.6. Setting (location and concept of the programme)

The seven Case Studies (of which three are included in this publication) identify three characteristics as being most significant if the programme is to achieve its aims; being young person centred, being flexible and being open (transparent).

In addition the young person should have a right to contribute to making decisions through participation as much as possible. The Setting form should be tailored to the needs of the young person and it must be possible to respond quickly when these needs change. In relation to this it is very important to consider and plan for transition (beginning and end of the programme, programme change).

The choice of programme for Lena was motivated primarily by the need for protection and the planning for her transition to and arrival at the programme is hardly mentioned in the files. On the other hand, her return to Germany was well planned, the German care worker met Lena in Portugal and spent some time there before returning with her to Germany. Lena was also able to take her dog which meant that they had to travel by road.

With Christian the first choice of programme in the Supported Group proved to be inappropriate but his later care in Italy was tailored to his development needs.

In addition the setting must be flexible and open to take advantage of every small opportunity. For André, in the beginning a residential and individual social learning programme was chosen because the support services felt, with good evidence, that as a 16-year-old he should not live alone. André, however chose to live initially on the street. The decision then was to choose a very hands off form of ambulant care (hotel and street) with the disadvantage that it was much more difficult to control. This led to a need for a high level of ambulant care.

The chance to join a programme in Italy away from his familiar milieu and dependent on his care workers gave Christian the first real possibility to change his pattern of withdrawing.

The location of the programme is not alone the most important success factor. The personal skills and level of experience of the care worker is crucial as is the fit between the care Worker and Young Person (so-called matching). The effectiveness of the Setting is closely connected to the personality of the Carer, their attachment behaviour and the quality of their relationship. These criteria are implicit in the choice of programme.

Lena found security in the normal family life of the care worker couple, Christian met an intellectual care worker and found the master that he sought. André was presented with a care worker who could give him boundaries and through them security.

Using Lena as an example, the group discussion time and again revolved around the idea that therapy was the only cure available if pedagogic means (or the care workers) meet their limits.

There isn't so much evidence in the case studies that this is the case. The care workers were able to provide an emotional foundation through sensitive support so that further therapeutic steps towards dealing with traumatic experiences can be taken. A programme which focussed solely on therapy appeared, on the other hand, to not be very promising.

In summary the following four factors contribute to a successful Setting:

- Effective matching between the care worker(s) and young person (including a fit in line with attachment theory and a mutual liking)

- The existence of smallest common denominators
- The flexibility and adaptability of the Setting to changing needs and stages of development of the cared for.
- Ensuring that there are 'emotional safe havens' beyond the programme's duration.

5.7. Cooperation amongst stakeholders

5.7.1. Youth Welfare Office

The three case studies in the English version of this publication provide little information about the quality of the relationship between the service provider and the Youth Welfare Office.

Examination of all seven case studies shows that the working relationship is always considered to be a positive one when the Youth Welfare Office is able to accept the suggestions of the service provider and when transferrals from one case worker to the next were successful. On the other hand, if responsibilities were not clearly assigned within the Youth Welfare Office, cooperation with the case workers suffered.

In one example, it was felt that the decision to abruptly terminate a programme in a foreign country had no pedagogic foundation and was more likely to be financial. On the whole, the quality of cooperation between Youth Welfare Office and the service provider seem to have a reciprocal effect on the amount of progress made in the programme.

5.7.2. Service provider – care worker

Retrospectively, the Care Workers and the coordinators rate their collaboration as positive on the whole. The Coordinators valued the work that the care workers were doing. For the care workers it was important that the Coordinators took time on their visits. There was a slight undertone that the care workers felt that their commitment should be more recognised, for example Christian's care worker in their rating of the cooperation between themselves and the Coordinator.

In hindsight the coordinator could have shown more initiative and provided the care worker with more opportunities to retreat within firmer boundaries.

André had a pair of care workers (one male, one female). This was not free of conflict and this led, in the end, to the female care worker leaving. This led, in turn to André having to deal with the separation and face issues concerning his mother with which he had not yet dealt with. Here also, the Coordinator might have played a stronger part.

The dual role of the Coordinator who was somebody who was there for both the young person and the care worker was criticised in the group discussion.

Lena raised it as an issue in her interviews, that she found it very difficult when the Coordinator wanted to speak to the care worker alone and she had no opportunity to 'defend' herself. In critical situations the Coordinator must be intensely aware of the double role and be able to provide coaching as well as supervision.

5.7.3. The care worker and other support services / institutions

There is a wide and diverse net of support services including the police and psychiatric hospitals which often become involved. It is certainly helpful in these cases to avoid the use of threats as, for example, happened with Christian in the first programme location. It is better to collaborate to achieve more fruitful outcomes. This holds also true for schools, therapists or other stakeholders such as André's hotel chef. In order to do this the service provider and care workers should network and emphasise the importance of this aspect to the young people. The characteristics could be described as such:

- It would be valuable if Coordinators could be trained in attachment theory or at the very least, received regular clarification of, and reflection on, the task.
- More clarity over the degree to which the Youth Welfare Office determines the design of the programme and who, from the Youth Welfare Office is ultimately responsible.
- The coordinators are both supervisor and coaches for the care workers. The care worker should ensure that they approach the Coordinators for help and offers. Case supervision (that is advice and reflexion conducted by a supervisor) should be standard offering for all care workers.
- If there is more than one care worker working in a family, they must be well coordinated and, additionally to case supervision, team supervision should be encouraged.
- Communication and cooperation could be improved by developing a network of personal contacts within the relevant external organisations

6. A view – aspects of attachment theory in individual social educational (pedagogic) work and research

It became increasingly clear as the research progressed that young people in receipt of individual social educational types of care are burdened by very difficult biographies which in most cases lead to severe attachment difficulties.

The research team had very active discussions about this and the authors reached the conclusion that individual social education and research in this area on the subject of attachment cannot be mutually exclusive.

If you wanted to name the most important method used to work with traumatised young people with some or many attachment problems then it would be attachment theory.

Attachment theory was developed by the English psychoanalyst John Bowlby and combines clinical psychoanalysis with evolutionary biology. According to this theory, attachment is the special relationship of a person to their parent or carer. It is that band, characterised by feeling, which ties an individual over time to another specific person.[24]

This secure band, this attachment can be established in early years by a sensitive primary carer. In the most cases this is the mother. Today it is thought that it can be several people.[25]

The better the carer looks after the child, the more stable and more secure the attachment patterns will be that the child develops and which can subsequently be accessed again and again.

According to Mary Ainsworth sensitive behaviour is made up of these four building blocks:

---

24   Vgl. M.D.S. Ainsworth (1973)

25   ⏋ J.A. Chambers, K.G. Power, N. Loucks, V. Swanson (2000)

- Be aware of the child's communications
- interpret them right
- respond appropriately and
- immediately

When children have such a more or less sensitive person around them in their early years, they internalise a feeling of security that forms an inner representation which they keep and can rely on in times of stress. This behaviour in times of stress, the attachment behaviour, is fundamental to a positive development. If this is not available to a child, their development takes place in very much more difficult conditions.[26]

The young people who come to "Jugendhilfe Phöinix e. V." or other organisations providing the same services suffer under these difficult conditions. They have often experienced mistreatment and abuse instead of protection and security. They have experienced neglect instead of respectful care. They have learnt that closeness is not the same as security and that the things that they have had to survive have forced them to adopt strategies which they and their environment find difficult to endure.

When Lena prefers to wander the dark streets at night instead of sleeping in her flat or when Christian explores 'the dark side' and sees himself as a wandering threat dressed in a black leather coat and carrying a sword, these are survival strategies which seek to retain some control over a situation which would otherwise be too threatening.

To stay with Lena: If a child experiences her own bed, which should be a cosy haven of security as a place of horror why should this child, or later as a teenager in residential care trust that they are safe

---

26 Cp. K. Grossmann, K. Grossmann (2012), S. 637 ff. cp. : K. H. Heinz Brisch / T. Hellbrügge (2003), S. 105ff.

and that they can trust? Lena's care worker was aware of this and could take account of it despite her challenging behaviour.

When André lost his mother at the age of four and nobody discussed it with him, when he was left with a father who was completely overwhelmed and who used the clip around the ear as a means of bringing up his child, then the support services cannot expect that he trusts adults or is open for ideas of harmony and structure.

On the contrary these young people break all known limits, particularly when things happen which cannot be explained by the young person then their own logic forces them into destructive behaviour. As an example may serve the sudden departure of the female care worker in Andre's case.

Here it is helpful if the personalities of the care workers encourage (from the point of view of attachment theory) the young persons to help develop their emotional maturity.

In order for any of the identified characteristics of a successful programme, like 'participation' 'Setting', or 'working on the biography' to have a positive impact, there must first be a connection between the Carer and the Cared for, that at least has the potential to develop emotional maturity. The experience of attachment would, ideally, quasi be re-experienced and the patterns of attachment which already existed in the mind of the toddler would be overlaid by a succession of positive experiences of alternative behaviours.

'Sensitivity'[27] is not only with small children of advantage but also in living with young people. The care worker couple in Portugal were able, intuitively, to allow Lena to approach them and to spend all of their available time to get to know her.

In summary, attachment theory can be applied to or transferred to youth welfare work when the four paradigms (perceive – interpret – respond promptly and appropriately) from Mary Ainsworth (in modified form) are applied to the care of young people:

---

[27] M.D.S. Ainsworth (1973)

- **The perception of the condition of the young person,** that means that the care worker has their eye on the young person, is mentally alert and who is sensitive to their surroundings
- **Appropriate interpretation of what the young person communicates** which is not coloured by the interests of the care worker
- **A prompt and timely response** which allows the young person to understand the connection between their action and the response of the care worker. A prompt response induces a feeling of the consequences of one's actions and what one is communicating in contrast to the feeling of helplessness when the behaviour is met with no response.
- **An appropriate reaction** that gives the young person what they need. Appropriate means what suits the age and stage of development of the young person and the situation.

In order to make use of these paradigms certain conditions need to be met, described here as six criteria

- **to really see the young person** to seek to discover their *real needs* and to talk to the young person in a non-judgemental way. This includes accepting the young person as they are. When the young person exhibits behaviour (like Christian with his sword and leather jacket) which is difficult to endure then to seek possible ways of changing the conditions. In Italy it was neither necessary nor indeed pleasant to walk around wearing those items.
- **To recognise the suffering of the young person,** be prepared to deal with the history of the young person and seek to understand.
- **Show some of the private aspects of your life to the young person,** even a young person understands their Carer better

when he/she knows a little about the context in which they move, which may also mean that the care worker must show some more vulnerable aspects of their personality.
- **Build trust** by being **dependable** in what you says and do, particularly in difficult situations.
- **To resist the impulse (and sometimes the wish) to start an (unequal) power struggle**
- **An attitude that allows you to continuously reflect on your own behaviour**

This attitude should be internalised so that it forms part of the practical everyday contact with the young person. This provides the decisive foundations for a successful care worker relationship.

The work with young people with very difficult biographies as part of an individual programme based on attachment theory is dependent on a compatibility between the attachment behaviour of the care worker and that of the young person, especially in situations causing anxiety, stress or other conflicts.

This so called 'matching' of care worker and young person based on their styles of attachment behaviour could – an hypothesis of the one of the authors of this research – play a significant role in the success or failure for 1:1 care in youth welfare programmes. That would mean that prior to establishing a programme in the future a more differentiated assessment of both the attachment behaviour of the young person AND that of the intended care worker is carried out to determine the potential for development for the young person on the basis of more or less compatible attachment behaviours.

Future research could explore further the hypothesis of Matching.

List of references

Ainsworth, M. D. S. (1973): The development of infant-mother attachment, In: Caldwell, B. M. / Riciutti, H. (Hg.): Review of child development research Bd. 3. Chicago, S. 1-94.

AIM Arbeitskreis individualpädagogischer Maßnahmen NRW e. V. (2007): Evaluationsstudie. Jugendliche in individualpädagogischen Maßnahmen. Durchgeführt vom Institut des Rauhen Hauses. Hamburg.

Baierl, Marin (2010): Herausforderung Alltag. Praxishandbuch für die pädagogische Arbeit mit psychisch gestörten Jugendlichen. 2. Aufl. Vandenhoeck & Ruprecht Verlag Göttingen.

Brisch, K. H. (2003): Bindungsstörungen und Trauma. Grundlagen für eine gesunde Bindungsentwicklung. In: Brisch K. H. / Hellbrügge, T. (2003) (Hg.): Bindung und Trauma. Risiken und Schutzfaktoren für die Entwicklung von Kindern. Klett-Cotta Stuttgart, S. 105-135

Chambers, J. A. / Power, K. G. / Loucks, N. / Swanson, V. (2000): Psychometric properties of the Parental Bonding Instrument and its association with psychological distress in a group of incarcerated young offenders in Scotland. In: Social Psychiatry and Psychiatric Epidemiology No. 35. Springer Verlag Berlin, S. 318–325.

Dettenborn, H. (2010): Kindeswohl und Kindeswille. Psychologische und rechtliche Aspekte. Ernst Reinhardt Verlag München.

Fischer, T. / Ziegenspeck, J. W. (2009): Betreuungsreport Ausland. Verlag Edition Erlebnispädagogik Lüneburg.

Flick, U. (2010): Design und Prozess qualitativer Forschung. In: Flick, U. / von Kardoff, E. / Steinke, I. (2010): Was ist qualitative Forschung? In: Flick, U. / von Kardof, E. / Steinke, I. (Hg.): Qualitative Forschung. Rowohlt Verlag Reinbek bei Hamburg, S. 252-265

Flick, U. / von Kardoff, E. / Steinke, I. (2010): Was ist qualitative Forschung? In: Flick, U. / von Kardof, E. / Steinke, I. (Hg.): Qualitative Forschung. Rowohlt Verlag Reinbek bei Hamburg, S. 13-29.

Fröhlich-Gildhoff, K. (2003): Einzelbetreuung in der Jugendhilfe. Lit Verlag Münster-Hamburg-London.

Grossmann, K. / Grossmann, K. (2012) (Hg.): Bindungen. Das Gefüge psychischer Sicherheit. 5. vllst. über. Aufl. Klett-Cotta Stuttgart.

Hüther, G. (2003): Die Auswirkungen traumatischer Erfahrungen im Kindesalter auf die Hirnentwicklung. In: Brisch K. H. /

Hellbrügge, T. (2003) (Hg.): Bindung und Trauma. Risiken und Schutzfaktoren für die Entwicklung von Kindern. Klett-Cotta Stuttgart, S. 94-104

von Kardoff, E. (2010): Qualitative Evaluationsforschung. In: Flick, U. / von Kardoff, E. / Steinke, I. (Hg.): Qualitative Forschung. Rowohlt Verlag Reinbek bei Hamburg, S. 238-250.

Klawe, W. (2010): Verläufe und Wirkfaktoren individualpädagogischer Maßnahmen. Eine explorativ-rekonstruktive Studie. Im Auftrag der Bundesarbeitsgemeinschaft Individualpädagogik e. V. Durchgeführt vom Institut des Rauhen Hauses Hamburg.

Klein, J. / Arnold, J. / Macsenaere, M. (2011): InHAUS Individualpädagogische Hilfen im Ausland. Evaluation, Effektivität, Effizienz. Lambertus Verlag Freiburg.

Olk, T. (1986): Abschied vom Experten: Sozialarbeit auf dem Weg zu einer alternativen Professionalität. Dissertation. Juventa-Verl. Weinheim.

Otto, H.-U. / Polutta, A. / Ziegler, H. (2010): What Works. Welches Wissen braucht die soziale Arbeit? Verlag Barbara Budrich Opladen und Farmington Hills.

Riemann, J. (2012): Transfer in der Jugendhilfe oder: Was Kairos, Kassler und Sauerkraut miteinander zu tun haben. In: Ferstl, A. / Scholz, M. / Thiesen, C. (Hg.): Einsam und Gemeinsam. Sich und Menschen begegnen! ZIEL-Verlag Augsburg, S. 97-103

Schmidt, C. (2010): Analyse von Leitfadeninterviews. In: Flick, U. / von Kardoff, E. / Steinke, I. (Hg.): Qualitative Forschung. Rowohlt Verlag Reinbek bei Hamburg, S. 447-454.

Witte, M. D. (2009): Jugendliche in intensivpädagogischen Auslandsprojekten. Schneider Verlag Hohengehren Baltmannsweiler.

Appendix 1

Guidelines for Interviews
Interview Guideline Adolescents

Central Questions	Follow up
First of all please tell us about your current situation. What are you doing?	Housing, partnership/own family, school/training, employment, leisure time
If we went back in time (Google map, flight of birds, clock...) and you returned to the time when the programme at Jugendhilfe Phöinix e.V. started for you, what do you remember?	What images, sounds, smells do you remember from that time? Which person springs to mind? Which situations do you recall?
If you think even further back, how was it at that time? How was the decision made to start the programme at Jugendhilfe Phöinix e.V.	Do you have any idea now how you ended up in this situation? (Own situation – family situation) If you think back to that time: Are there any particular persons you recall in this context? (Child Protection Services, Jugendhilfe Phoenix, family) How was it for you at that time?

	Could you understand the decision? Were you involved in the decision?
	(Involvement, reasons)
Let us talk more closely about the programme.	Where was it? Who were your carers?
What do you recall about your time in your programme?	If you think of your Care Worker, what do you spontaneously remember? How did you feel about your Care Worker? How do you see this now?
There was someone at Jugendhilfe Phöinix responsible for you and the programme. Do you recall this person?	Do you know what this person was there for?
	What relevance did this person (the co-ordinator) have for you?
What else do you remember about your time with the programme which we have not mentioned yet?	For example: homesickness, conflict situations, nice moments, contact with mother or father (caution: absent parent!) contact with siblings, school...
	For example: How did the contact with your mother/your father take place? What was your experience of that?
	How do you see this today?
If you look back now to the	Did any particular experienc-

end of the programme: what was different from before? Are there any particular moments which you can remember from the programme? (If so:) Which moments are these?	es you have had with the programme help you later?
Current situation – How are you now?	Plans for the future?
Are there any questions which I did not ask you but which you would have liked to answer? You have now the opportunity to add these.	

Interview Guideline Parents

Central Questions	Follow up
What do you know about the current situation in the life of your child?	Housing, partnership/own family, school/training, employment, leisure time
Connection: If we go on a little journey back through time now (Google map, flight of birds, clock...) and you return to the time when the programme at Jugendhilfe Phöinix e.V. started for your son/your daughter, what do you remember?	What images, sounds, smells... do you remember from that time? Which person springs to mind? Which situations do you recall?
If you think further back, how was it at that time? How did it actually come to the decision for …… to start the programme at Jugendhilfe Phöinix e.V.	Do you have any idea how things did evolve in order for this decision to be made? (Family situation – situation of son/daughter) If you think back to that time: Are there any persons you recall in this context? (Child Protection Services, Jugendhilfe Phoenix, family) How was it for you at that time? Could you understand

		the decision? Did you have the feeling that you had been involved in the decision? (Involvement, reasons)
	I would like to look back to the time when you child was with the programme. What springs to mind if you think about the time with the programme?	If you think of the carers – what springs to mind spontaneously? How did you feel about the carer? How do you see this now?
	There was someone at Jugendhilfe Phöinix responsible for you and the programme. Do you recall this person?	Do you know what this person was there for? What relevance did this person (co-ordinator) have for you? What was helpful in the cooperation, what was obstructive?
	What was your experience with the workers of the Youth Welfare Office during the programme?	What was helpful, what was obstructive?
	What else do you recall about this time which we have not mentioned yet? What did you experience at this time?	For instance: And just how did the contact with your daughter/your son happen? What was your experience with that?

		How did you feel about the cooperation between the programme management and yourself? How do you see this today?
	And when you think back to the time when the programme ended: Which changes did you notice about your child? Where there any changes in your life at that time?	
	Current situation – How is your child today? And how are you?	Plans for the future of your child?
0	Are there any questions which I did not ask you but which you would have liked to answer? You have now the opportunity to add these.	

Interview Guideline Care Worker

Central Questions	Follow up
Initially I would like to ask you for some information about your programme.	Where? Specifics (offers, facilities)? Professional expertise and background experience of carers? Contact/cooperation on-site? Since when (at Jugendhilfe Phöinix e.V.)?
Now I would like you to think about the time before the admittance of X/Y into your programme Please describe which reasons led to the decision to place X/Y in your programme?	Who was involved? To what extend do you believe that X/Y could comprehend the decision or was involved respectively?
What spoke in favour of the admitting of X/Y into your programme, what against it? What moved you to accept the care of X/Y?	What was your specific offer to X/Y/ What do you believe made you/your programme suitable for X/Y?
If you recall you first meeting with X/Y/the first days and weeks: Which resources did you observe in X/Y?	ask about resources of youth and family resources
And now I would like you to let the course of the programme run before you inner eye in fast	What were the subjects of X/Y? What special challenges, achievements, crucial experienc-

	motion.	es or turning points do you recall?
		Which of your interventions/offers do you evaluate as especially helpful to X/Y?
		What was not going too well? With hindsight 6what what you do differently?
	How do you evaluate the cooperation with Jugendhilfe Phöinix e.V. (co-ordinator) in this particular case?	What was helpful, what was less helpful? What would you have wished differently?
	What did the contact to parents (to mother/to father) look like?	Caution: role of absent parent! To what extent could you involve, engage parents? What went well, where were difficulties?
	With what other experts did you cooperate during the programme? How would you evaluate this cooperation?	Coop. with school, recognised training provider/ apprenticeship, psychiatric ward, other public institutions...
	If you recall the end of the programme: how did this take place?	How was the end of the programme prepared/implemented?
	What do you believe had changed for X/Y through the programme?	How satisfied or dissatisfied had you been at termination of the programme?

	How do you asses X/Y's state of development at that time?	What feedback and by whom did you receive back than or in retrospect about your work with X/Y?
0	Are there any questions which I did not ask you but which you would have liked to answer? You have now the opportunity to add these.	
1	With what other experts did you cooperate during the programme? How would you evaluate this cooperation?	Coop. with school, recognised training company / apprenticeship, psychiatric ward, other public institutions...
2	If you recall the end of the programme: how did this take place?	How was the end of the programme prepared/implemented?
	What do you believe had changed for X/Y through the programme?	How satisfied or dissatisfied had you been at termination of the programme?
	How do you asses X/Y's state of development at that time?	What feedback and by whom did you receive back than or in retrospect about your work with X/Y?
3	Are there any questions which I did not ask you but which you would have liked to answer? You have now the opportunity to add these.	

Interview Guideline Coordination

Central Questions	Follow Up
Initially I would like you to recall the time before the admittance of X/Y into your programme Please describe which reasons led to the decision to place X/Y in your programme?	Who was involved? To what extend do you believe that X/Y could comprehend the decision or was involved respectively?
What spoke in favour of the admitting of X/Y into your programme, what against it? What moved you to accept the care of X/Y?	What was your specific offer to X/Y/ What do you believe made you/your programme suitable for X/Y?
If you recall you first meeting with X/Y/the first days and weeks: Which resources could you observe in X/Y?	ask about resources of youth and family resources
And now I would like you to let the course of the programme run before you inner eye in fast motion.	What were the subjects of X/Y? What special challenges, achievements, crucial experiences or turning points do you recall? Which of your interventions/offers of the carer do you evaluate as especially

	helpful to X/Y? From your point of view, what was not going too well?
How do you evaluate the cooperation between you and the carer in this particular case?	What was helpful, what was less helpful? What would you have wished differently?
What did the contact to parents (to mother/to father) look like?	Caution: role of absent parent! To what extent could you involve, engage parents? What went well, where were difficulties?
How was the cooperation with the Youth Welfare Office?	Ascertainment of needs – phrasing of application to Jugendhilfe Phöinix e.V. - organisation of professional cooperation of all involved – flexible updated support planning – termination of programme
If you recall the end of the programme: how did this take place? What do you believe had changed for X/Y through the programme? How do you asses X/Y's state of development at that time?	How was the end of the programme prepared/implemented? How satisfied or dissatisfied had you been at termination of the programme? What feedback and by whom did you receive back than or in retrospect about your work as coordinator?
Are there any questions which I did not ask you but which you would have liked to answer?	

You have now the opportunity to add these.	

Interview Guideline Youth Welfare Office

Central Questions	Follow Up
Initially I would like you to recall the time before the admittance of X/Y into your programme Please describe which reasons led to the decision to place X/Y in your programme?	Who was involved? To what extend do you believe that X/Y could comprehend the decision or was involved respectively?
What was in favour for admittance of X/Y into this programme, what was against?	What moved you to decide for admittance of X/Y at A?
	What was the specific offer of B to X/Y?/ What do you believe made this particular programme suitable for X/Y?
If you recall X/Y when he was admitted at Jugendhilfe Phöinix e.V.: Which resources could you observe on X/Y?	ask about resources of youth and family resources
And now I would like you to let the course of the programme run before you inner eye in fast motion.	What were the subjects of X/Y? What special challenges, achievements, crucial experiences or turning points do you recall?

	Which of your interventions/offers of the carer do you evaluate as especially helpful to X/Y? From your point of view, what was not going too well?
How do you evaluate the cooperation with Jugendhilfe Phöinix e.V.	What went well, what would you have wished differently?
What did the contact to parents (to mother/to father) look like?	Caution: role of absent parent! To what extent could you involve, engage parents? What went well, where were difficulties?
If you recall the end of the programme: how did this take place? What do you believe had changed for X/Y through the procedure? How do you asses X/Y's state of development at that time?	How was the end of the programme prepared/implemented? How satisfied or dissatisfied had you been at termination of the programme? What feedback and by whom did you receive back than or in retrospect about your work as leading agency worker?
Are there any questions which I did not ask you but which you would have liked to answer? You have now the opportunity to add these.	

The Authors

Jenne Riemann, b. 1958

lives in Hamburg (Germany), married and father of two children.

Qualified Social Education Worker (polytechnic), additional qualification in the field of experience education (Outward Bound), systematic and commitment based counselling and therapy.

Additional training for trauma therapy and trauma pedagogy
Child protection representative since 2013.

Active in youth welfare services for 20 years, conducted long-time programmes with adolescents (ambulant and residential)

Steffi Jöst, b. 1965

lives in Lindau (Germany), mother of a son.

Qualified Social Education Worker, Master of Business Administration (MBA), several additional qualifications including experience education at Outward Bound, management and leadership of social institutions, commitment based counselling and therapy as well as being a trained SAFE-Mentor (Secure Apprenticeship for Parents)

After a long-time activity as social education worker in the area of experience-educational travel programmes in Northern America, Canada and New Zealand as well as in southern Europe, she founded Jugendhilfe Phöinix e.V. in the year 1995. Management of the Jugendhilfe Phöinix e.V. which specialises on individual educational procedures home and abroad.

Catrin Fischer, b. 1965

lives in the Oderbruch (Germany), mother of two adult daughters.

Qualified Social Education Worker (polytechnic), systemic consultant (SG)
Professional experience in the areas of social planning, empiric social and practice research, occupational training, team and organisational development.
Since 2009 freelancing team coach, coach, lecturer, supervisor amongst others in youth welfare services.

Nicola Berchtold, b. 1973

lives in the south of France, mother of two children
Historian (MA).
Worked as assistant professor (University of Hamburg) as well as online journalist and part time for the administration at Jugendhilfe Phöinix e.V.
Through her partner, who works as adviser in individual educational youth welfare services, she was introduced to caring for young people in her own home.